THE
VIRTUOUS
WOMAN

Shattering the Superwoman Myth

Vicki Courtney

ISBN 0-6330-0760-9

This book is the text for course CG-0593 in the subject area Personal Life
of the Christian Growth Study Plan.

Dewey Decimal Classification: 248.843
Subject Heading: WOMEN/CHRISTIAN LIFE

Jon Rodda, Art Director
Jimmy Abegg, Photographer

To order additional copies of this resource: WRITE LifeWay Church Resources Customer Service;
One LifeWay Plaza; Nashville, TN 37234-0113; FAX order to (615) 251-5933; PHONE (800) 458-2772;
EMAIL to *customerservice@lifeway.com;* ORDER ONLINE at *www.lifeway.com;*
or VISIT the LifeWay Christian Store serving you.

Printed in the United States of America

Leadership and Adult Publishing
LifeWay Church Resources
One LifeWay Plaza
Nashville, TN 37234-0175

Table of Contents

About the Author

Vicki Courtney is author of *Virtuous Reality: Becoming the Ideal Woman* and a speaker to women of all ages. She is also the founder and Editor-in-Chief of an online Christian magazine for college women, *virtuousreality.com*.

A graduate of the University of Texas at Austin with a BA in Economics, Vicki became a Christian during her junior year while attending a conference for college students. She met her future husband Keith there, and he encouraged Vicki's discipleship. Her life before Christ greatly influences her writing and speaking as she seeks to be sensitive to women in the body of Christ as well as to those who still seek Him.

Vicki's greatest passion in ministry is to let women know God has equipped each of them with gifts and talents to be used for kingdom purposes. As women begin to see themselves through God's eyes, they will recognize the potential God has given them to impact lives in the great harvest.

Vicki resides in Austin with her husband Keith where she enjoys dating Keith, shopping with daughter Paige, and cheering for sons Ryan and Hayden in football, basketball, and baseball.

The Virtuous Woman

Becoming the Ideal Woman

about this study

In my years of teaching and speaking, I must admit that I have purposely avoided teaching on the Proverbs 31 woman. I mean, is this woman for real? She makes Martha Stewart look like a sluggard! If she really does exist, I'm not sure I would want to run in her circle. The two of us would not have much in common.

"Who can find a virtuous woman? for her price is far above rubies.

The heart of her husband doth safely trust in her, so that he shall have no need of spoil.

She will do him good and not evil all the days of her life.

She seeketh wool, and flax, and worketh willingly with her hands.

She is like the merchants' ships; she bringeth her food from afar.

She riseth also while it is yet night, and giveth meat to her household, and a portion to her maidens.

She considereth a field, and buyeth it: with the fruit of her hands she planteth a vineyard.

She girdeth her loins with strength, and strengtheneth her arms.

She perceiveth that her merchandise is good: her candle goeth not out by night.

She layeth her hands to the spindle, and her hands hold the distaff.

She stretcheth out her hand to the poor; yea, she reacheth forth her hands to the needy.

When I need a button sewn on a garment, I get out the Yellow Pages and flip to "S" for seamstress. I'm not even sure what "flax" is, and I'm curious as to whether "bringing her food in from afar" would include fast-food take-out.

The verse about having maidens is appealing. I was sure to point that one out to my husband. He was quick to point out a few other verses to me.

I could probably handle "buying a field," but would struggle with planting a vineyard when I can't even keep an ivy plant alive. Could "strengthening her arms" justify a membership to the local country club?

If I can't sew, can I hire someone else to "layeth hands to the spindle" and still get credit? Would "stretching out my hand to the poor" include participating in the canned food drive at my children's school?

She is not afraid of the snow for her household: for all her household are clothed with scarlet.

She maketh herself coverings of tapestry; her clothing is silk and purple.

Her husband is known in the gates when he sitteth among the elders of the land.

She maketh fine linen, and selleth it; and delivereth girdles unto the merchant.

Strength and honour are her clothing; and she shall rejoice in time to come.

She openeth her mouth with wisdom; and in her tongue is the law of kindness.

She looketh well to the ways of her household, and eateth not the bread of idleness.

Her children arise up, and call her blessed; her husband also, and he praiseth her.

Many daughters have done virtuously, but thou excellest them all.

Favour is deceitful, and beauty is vain: but a woman that feareth the Lord, she shall be praised.

Give her of the fruit of her hands; and let her own works praise her in the gates."

Proverbs 31:10-31 (KJV)

If her children are "clothed in scarlet" and she in "silk and purple" does this give me permission to shop at the finest stores and charge it?

Does when she "opens her mouth with wisdom and kindness," include times when her children are fighting and the toilets need cleaning?

Does "eateth not the bread of idleness" mean that I must give up my 15-minute power nap in the afternoon?

Did her children and husband "arise up and call her blessed" every single day? How did she manage that? Did she withhold food on the days they refused?

Does "beauty is vain" mean I must give up my manicured nails and natural blonde highlights? Last of all, what exactly does it mean to "feareth the Lord"?

For years, Christian women have struggled to understand what this woman is all about. Reading this passage can evoke more guilt than eating a one-pound bag of M&M's. Is she considered the "ideal woman" and, if so, should we seek to emulate her many qualities? Is the Proverbs 31 passage still timely for today, or is it an outdated fixture of the past? Is there hope for those of us who don't make biscuits from scratch or sew our own clothes?

Regardless of the confusion this passage has generated, one truth remains: By no accident did this passage get included in God's Holy Word. The virtuous woman is a rare find in today's world. I don't know about you, but the thought of becoming a woman who "excels them all," is rather appealing to me. I have a long way to go, so consider me a fellow sojourner as together we seek to unravel the mystery behind this virtuous woman. In the end, may we each find the pursuit to be worth the effort.

Vicki Courtney

session one

The Ideal Woman

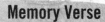

Memory Verse

"For my thoughts are not your thoughts, neither are your ways my ways," declares the Lord. "As the heavens are higher than the earth, so are my ways higher than your ways and my thoughts than your thoughts."

Isaiah 55:8-9

This Week's Lessons

Day 1
What's Your Legacy?

Day 2
Proverbs 31:
Ideal or Unreal?

Day 3
The World's Ideal Woman

Day 4
How Do YOU
Measure Up?

Day 5
Preparing for the Pursuit

From birth, we struggle to find our place in this world. Consciously or not, we search for identity, worth, and purpose. Somewhere along the way, our definition of the "ideal woman" begins to form, molded by the influences around us. We set out to reach the standards imposed by our definition. The effects will be felt for generations to come.

Have you ever wished for a formula, a road map, or instructional booklet to guide you in the pursuit to become the ideal woman? Well, I have good news: There is one! God's Word is still timely for today. He has not left us in the world to figure everything out on our own. What an awesome thought that the very words we read on His pages are God-breathed and inspired for such a time as this. It is our manual for living. Everything we need, including a formula for identity, worth, and purpose, is provided in the pages of His Word. Without it, we would be lost.

When it comes to a definition of the ideal woman, many opinions exist. I believe God is calling women to measure these definitions against a proved standard–His standard. May we be open to what He shows us in the weeks to come, as He shines the light of His Truth on what it takes for us to become the ideal woman in His eyes.

Note: The woman in Proverbs 31 was a wife and mother, but the character we seek applies to all women, whether married or single, with or without children. If you are single, or not a mother, please don't be put off by the occasional reference to husband or children. The goal of this study is to encourage all women in the pursuit to become virtuous women. You will quickly find that this study emphasizes the ability of the Proverbs 31 woman to center her entire life around her relationship with God, not to define herself by her life situation.

Day 1

What's Your Legacy?

Imagine viewing your own funeral. You are sitting in the back of the room, undetected as friends and loved ones come up one by one to say a few words about your life. Your husband, children, grandchildren, pastor, co-worker, and a neighbor summarize in paragraphs what your life was all about. What will they say? Will you be remembered for your contributions in the work force? Will you be remembered for donating money to worthy causes? Will you be remembered as a friend to the friendless? Will you be remembered for your tireless devotion to the local church?

Your entire life has pointed to this very moment, and before your eyes, your legacy begins to unfold. Qualities you possessed on earth will be molded into stories and memories and handed down to future generations. Your entire existence will be summed up with words describing who you were as a person, what you accomplished, and the legacy you leave behind. You begin to weep as you realize that your life is but a small speck on the timeline of eternity. Do you weep with tears of joy or regret as this truth begins to sink in? Would you do things differently if given another chance?

Fortunately, it's not too late. Now is the time to think about the legacy you will someday leave. Who you are today will impact who you are tomorrow. Are you in pursuit of developing qualities that will someday mold a legacy you can be proud of? Will you later realize that worldly success was the wrong goal to pursue?

Are you pursuing God's goals for your life? ❑ Yes ❑ Not Sure ❑ No

Read the statement in the margin. Is it a comforting thought or is it a disturbing thought? Why?

_____

_____

You are who you've been becoming.

In regard to qualities you possess, what statements would you someday hope to hear by the following?

Your husband:_____

_____

_____

Your children: _____

_____

_____

Your pastor:_____

_____

_____

Your friends: _____

_____

_____

Your coworkers: _____

_____

_____

You will only get one chance at this life—with no dress rehearsal. Believe it or not, the legacy you leave behind can impact your family's lineage for generations to come. Many women fail to take this responsibility seriously. We live in a pleasure-seeking world that stresses instant gratification. Many people give little thought to developing qualities that will impact our own future, much less future generations.

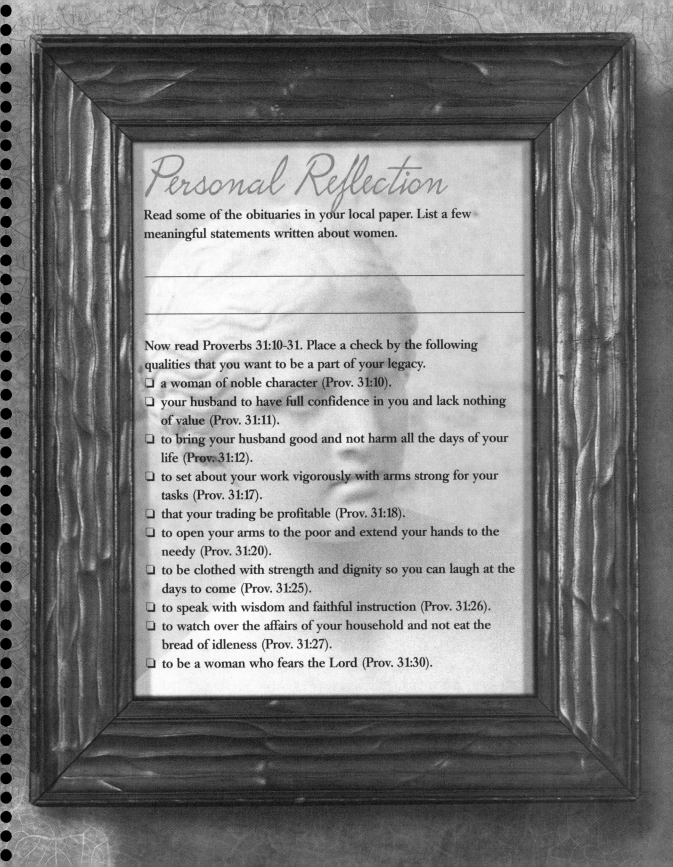

Personal Reflection

Read some of the obituaries in your local paper. List a few meaningful statements written about women.

_____

_____

Now read Proverbs 31:10-31. Place a check by the following qualities that you want to be a part of your legacy.

❏ a woman of noble character (Prov. 31:10).

❏ your husband to have full confidence in you and lack nothing of value (Prov. 31:11).

❏ to bring your husband good and not harm all the days of your life (Prov. 31:12).

❏ to set about your work vigorously with arms strong for your tasks (Prov. 31:17).

❏ that your trading be profitable (Prov. 31:18).

❏ to open your arms to the poor and extend your hands to the needy (Prov. 31:20).

❏ to be clothed with strength and dignity so you can laugh at the days to come (Prov. 31:25).

❏ to speak with wisdom and faithful instruction (Prov. 31:26).

❏ to watch over the affairs of your household and not eat the bread of idleness (Prov. 31:27).

❏ to be a woman who fears the Lord (Prov. 31:30).

The Proverbs 31 woman left quite a legacy. We'll talk more about her and seek to understand her attributes. As you close in prayer, ask God to help you improve the qualities you want to be a part of your legacy.

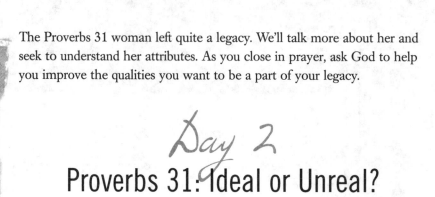

Day 2
Proverbs 31: Ideal or Unreal?

I'll never forget the first time I read Proverbs 31 as a new believer. Before becoming a Christian, I was a feminist, strongly opposed to the Christian faith. My mother, a successful career woman, earned her law degree in her 40s, and she taught me I could accomplish anything I put my mind to. I set out to emulate her success and pave a similar path.

My pursuit turned when a friend invited me to a church-sponsored retreat during my junior year in college. The gospel was presented; I wrestled over whether to trust Christ. On about the 11th stanza of "I Have Decided to Follow Jesus," I gave my heart and life to Jesus Christ. I shared my decision with another student who took time to encourage me in my faith and emphasized discipleship's importance.

I was awed by this man's commitment to the Lord and we became fast friends. When I married this wonderful man, I became June Cleaver's daughter-in-law. A full-time homemaker, she has more recipes than I have brain cells. My husband claims she took breakfast requests and whipped up something different for each person. If my kids tried that, I'd hand each an apron and tell them to go for it.

Imagine my shock when I read Proverbs 31. I wanted desperately to please my heavenly Father, not to mention my new husband. I futilely attempted to live up to this passage and emulate her long list of domestic skills. No sooner could I prepare a meal without setting off the fire alarm, I discovered we were expecting our first child. Thirteen months after we were married, I also became a full-time mother. I cringed at the mention of the Proverbs 31 woman. She was everything I was not. The more I heard about her, the less confident I felt as a Christian wife and mother. In my lack of understanding, my attitude began to sour.

What had women done to deserve such a difficult lot? Surely there had to be more to life than rejoicing with a friend over a new method to remove spit-up stains from a bib. Now don't get me wrong here, I *love* being a mother. When my children were babies I loved rocking them until they fell asleep in my arms. I loved getting on the floor and playing with them, making up silly songs, and tickling them to make them laugh. However, it quickly became clear that being creative with the kids didn't get the toilets cleaned and the beds made. It never seemed to be enough, and I perceived that reaching Proverbs 31 status was based more on an ability to perform domestic chores than to make a baby laugh.

The more frustrated I became, the more I wondered what my life might have been like had I pursued a path that highlighted my talents more. I was torn between the world's ideal woman and God's virtuous woman. Could I find fulfillment in living God's way? If I invested everything I had into becoming the "ideal woman" as defined by God, would that be a legacy I could be proud of someday?

Read Proverbs 31:10-31. Which verses did you find most intimidating?

_____

Can you relate to my frustration of trying to live up to the Proverbs 31 woman's standards? ❏ Yes ❏ No ❏ Somewhat

What are you feeling right now, in regard to the Proverbs 31 woman?
❏ Just call me June Cleaver.　　❏ This fits my mother to a T!
❏ The woman has ADD.　　　　❏ I'm never reading that passage again.
　 Get her some Ritalin, fast.　❏ I like a good challenge.

What top five qualities did the Proverbs 31 woman possess (in your opinion) that lent to her virtuous standing and made her a woman who "surpassed them all" (Prov. 31:29)?

1. _____　4. _____

2. _____　5. _____

3. _____

Day 3
The World's Ideal Woman

Most women follow the world's influence. Becoming a Christian does not exempt us from its influences, especially those of us who look to the world for worth, identity, and purpose. I know; I have been this woman. The pressure to live up to the world's expectations continued to plague me after I became a Christian, contributing, I believe, to an eating disorder I struggled with in past years. We must examine what influenced our thinking or we may suffer the consequences.

What do you feel is the world's definition of the ideal woman?

_____

I asked my church's college department to define the ideal woman according to the world. After reassuring the males they would not be lynched, they shared what many young men consider the ideal woman to be. The bottom line? Many young men feel the ideal woman possesses beauty, brains, bucks, and a great body! Unfortunately, the answers remain much the same when polling men and women of all ages.

Read 1 Samuel 16:1-7. According to verse 7, at what does man look?

_____

At what does God look? _____

Which do you honestly notice—a person's appearance or their heart?

_____

How might 1 Samuel 16:7 relate to many women's quest to become the world's ideal woman?

_____

In the following activity mark an X on each line to indicate approximately where you would rank according to the world's standard.

Beauty:

It's what's on the inside that counts, right?	Supermodels hate me, I'm so beautiful.

Brains:

I wish I had some.	I could explain photosynthesis at the age of 3.

Body:

Unfortunately, I do have one.	Every summer I look forward to swimsuit shopping.

Bucks:

Aren't those male deer?	Bill Gates calls me to borrow money.

How we define the ideal woman starts when we are young. For many, exposure to the world's definition of the ideal woman began at home. Some women were told to look pretty, lose weight, make straight A's, and pursue an education that would lend itself to making a good living. Others were exposed to parents living at breakneck speed to prove themselves to a world that is often hard to please. Some had the good fortune to receive training on what it is to be a virtuous woman.

What positive and negative messages about becoming an ideal woman did you receive in your early years?

too overwhelming

Even if parents do their best to stress virtuous qualities, children discover what qualities the world applauds. The world is loud and clear about the ideal woman. The media, magazines, the movie industry, and others bombard us with their opinions of the ideal woman.

What messages did you receive from others during your early years?
(Example: Drill team coach told you to lose weight.)

_____

Do you feel you have been influenced in any way by the world's messages
in regard to the ideal woman? ❑ Yes ❑ Not Sure ❑ No

How? _____

Pay attention to the messages around you today. List any that support the
world's definition of the ideal woman.

_____

Reread this week's memory verse. Ask God to show you His thoughts and
ways in defining the ideal woman.

Day 4
How Do YOU Measure Up?

Just for fun, I asked my daughter Paige and her friend what they thought
the ideal (perfect) woman was like. They responded: blonde hair and blue
eyes (interestingly, a description of themselves), mom-like, not strict,
athletic, smart, punctual, persnickety (whatever that is), likes pets, playful,
interesting, lots of hobbies, sensitive, outgoing, tan, average-length hair,
freckles on her nose, medium height, petite, flexible with her schedule,
cooks, cleans, smiles, Christianlike, goes to church, divides her time right,
doesn't leave anyone out or take sides, prays and reads the Bible every day,
always knows what to do, comforts people when they are sad, trustworthy,
polite, honest, married, and never fights with her husband.

Overall, I was impressed at the quantity of internal attributes they listed. I
thought it interesting that they never mentioned "pretty" or "beautiful," but
instead listed specific physical characteristics. I was surprised that their
answers were so specific in regard to appearance. I can only imagine their

answers in 10 years! Amazingly, without knowledge of the Proverbs 31 woman, they touched on many of her qualities.

What if we compiled a description of the world's ideal woman? Might the list include: independent, self-reliant, self-sufficient, confident, productive, beautiful, professional, intelligent, successful, and slender. This woman looks out for #1 and isn't afraid to be assertive. She can have a career and a family. She is superwoman. She does it all and she does it well. She is at soccer games with her laptop and PTA meetings with her cell phone. She always looks polished and never seems tired. She takes off work to drive on field trips or to take cupcakes to school on her child's birthday. She has spent enough quality time with her children that they share their innermost thoughts and dreams with her. They never complain if she lacks time for them because they are proud of her.

I can honestly tell you that in my 36 years of living, I have never met a woman who has been successful in meeting the above standard. Most women who attempt it are in therapy and popping Prozac like it's candy.

Have you ever attempted to meet the world's standard of the ideal woman?
❑ Yes ❑ Not Sure ❑ No

The following might help you take a more introspective look at yourself. Answer (T)rue or (F)alse.

____ I worry more about fat grams than having a daily quiet time.
____ I would not have a problem going out in public without my makeup.
____ My first thought in the morning is, "where is my Bible?" not "what should I wear today?"
____ I would feel more self-worth if I were successful in the business world.
____ Looking at a lingerie catalog throws me into a major depression.
____ A bad hair day can affect my whole mood.
____ I would rather someone say I am kind-hearted than pretty.
____ I am able to look in a full-length mirror while wearing my swimsuit and say, "I am fearfully and wonderfully made."

OK, you have to admit—that last one is a killer. I have made some progress, but it tends to come out through clenched teeth and a really fake smile.

Before we can embrace a biblical model of the ideal woman, we must be willing to question the world's definition. You may have laughed when checking the survey, but the truth is, it is serious. Women molded by the world's definition of the ideal woman can experience devastating consequences if their worth is misdefined. We will discuss self-worth in week 3, but we must first dispel the world's definition of the ideal woman.

Look up each of the following verses and describe in your own words how it relates to the worldly pursuit to become the ideal woman:

Matthew 16:26:_____

_____

1 Corinthians 3:19a:_____

_____

1 John 2:15:_____

_____

1 John 2:16:_____

_____

Perhaps your ideal woman closely aligns with the Proverbs 31 woman's skills. Maybe your comfort zone is the kitchen, and you're known for your flaky pie crusts. Maybe you just whipped up matching mother-daughter frocks for the church banquet that you planned from start to finish. Perhaps you just faux-finished all the walls in your house and you are the picture of domesticity. Does it take these things to become the ideal woman?

Next week we'll begin to focus on key internal attributes that contributed to the virtuous standing of the Proverbs 31 woman. More importantly, these attributes made her a "woman who surpasses them all" (Prov. 31:29). Perhaps you're well on your way to becoming the ideal woman in God's eyes and this Bible study will be the encouragement you need in this worthy pursuit. Who doesn't want to become such a woman?

Day 5
Preparing for the Pursuit

When I write or speak, I consider the parable of the sower, what I call the "Scattered Seed Principle." It basically assumes God's truth is put forth (the scattered seed) and only a fraction will fall onto good soil. I wrote this study for those women whose hearts are prepared and as a result, whose lives will produce thirty-, sixty-, or a hundred-fold what has been sown.

Read Matthew 13:1-23. Note: If you are grumbling that there are 23 verses, let me warn you–this is not a good sign! What four types of ground does Jesus describe?

1. _____ 3. __hard soil__

2. __weeds__ 4. __good soil__

The sower can be anyone who comes with the good news of Jesus Christ. The seed is the message about the kingdom, but could also refer to any truth presented from God's Word. Keep in mind that the ground to which Jesus refers represents the hearts of the people who will hear His truth.

What hinders growth in the first type of ground? _____

Satan probably finds seed lying on this ground often. Because it has never been tilled, it provides fast-food for an enemy on the run.

What can be done to soften this type of heart for the seed to take root?

_____

What hinders growth in the second type of ground? _____

Though this soil received the seed with enthusiasm, the roots can't penetrate due to the rocks and the shallow soil. When trouble or persecution comes, the sun scorches the young plant and snuffs out any progress.

> "Search me, O God, and know my heart; test me and know my anxious thoughts. See if there is any offensive way in me, and lead me in the way everlasting."
>
> Psalm 139:23-24

What can be done to prepare this type of heart for deeper roots and prevent any progress from being stifled by times of adversity?

_____

What hinders growth in the third type of ground? _____

This seed takes root and grows a bit, only to be choked out later by thorns.

How can the "cares of the world" and the "deceitfulness of wealth" hinder growth of God's truth in a human heart?

_____

What hinders growth in the fourth type of ground? _____

We are not to assume that the good soil was free from stones and thorns. This heart is prepared in spite of the hindrances, due to proper advance soil preparation. As a result, it will receive seed that is sown upon it.

How might one prepare his or her heart to receive the seed?

_____

My heart has been represented by all four types of ground. Today it is the good soil, but that does not assure me that it will be tomorrow. I must do everything I can to keep my heart fertile and receptive to God's truth. The key? An active prayer life and staying in God's Word daily will fertilize every type of soil to produce growth.

Which of the four types of ground best represents your heart?
❏ hard   ❏ shallow   ❏ overgrown   ❏ good

Hearts represented by the good soil did not get there by accident but by the sovereign act of the Holy Spirit acting through persons' labor. By an act of their will, they labored long and hard to have this type of heart. Read the verse in the margin. What fruit will be reaped and from whom?

_____

"*Sow for yourselves righteousness, reap the fruit of unfailing love, and break up your unplowed ground, for it is time to seek the Lord, until he comes and showers righteousness on you.*"

Hosea 10:12

Only by seeking the Lord will we be able to break up the unplowed ground and soften our hearts to receive God's truth. We are motivated to change because the unfailing love of God the Father compels us.

Recently I got a good chuckle over a conversation between my son, Ryan, and his buddy, Garrett. Garrett was explaining to Ryan he had seen a survey of jobs and the average salary for each. He told Ryan, "When I get out of college, I'm going to find a job as a CEO. I don't know what they do, but they sure make a lot of money."

Becoming a woman who surpasses them all is a similar pursuit. Many women want to reach this status, but few are willing to put forth the time and effort required. Becoming a woman who surpasses them all is a lifelong journey. The material we will cover in the weeks to come is radical. It may require change. I know that's a word we don't like to hear, but I want to be honest with you from the beginning.

If you are looking for a "quick-fix" Bible study, this isn't it. I am not content to simply become a "woman who does noble things." I want to leave a legacy that will impact generations to come. I want my husband and children to arise and call me blessed. I want to become a woman who surpasses them all. I want my works to bring me praise at the city gate. I want these things because God wants them for me.

The truths I am writing about have changed my life. I want them to change yours too. I won't tell you only what you want to hear. Do you want to know what made the Proverbs 31 woman different? Are you willing to do what it takes to become this type of woman? The fact that you are studying about the virtuous woman speaks well of your desires and intentions. I pray God will use this resource as a tool to start you in your pursuit to become a virtuous woman or to confirm that you are on the right track already. For this to happen, you must be spiritually prepared.

On a piece of paper or card you can carry with you, write a prayer to God, sharing what type of heart you hope to have. If necessary, ask Him to break up the unplowed ground and soften your heart. Commit to pray this throughout this study.

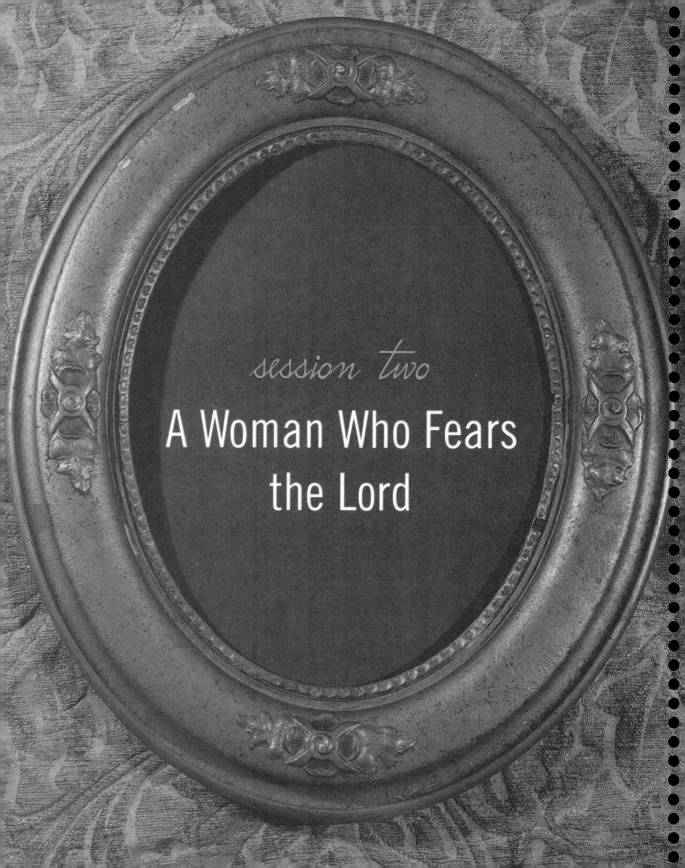

session two

A Woman Who Fears the Lord

*"From everlasting to everlasting the Lord's love
is with those who fear him, and his righteousness
with their children's children—with those who keep
his covenant and remember to obey his precepts."*

Psalm 103:17-18

V
I
T
Fea**R** of the Lord
U
E

This Week's Lessons

Day 1
Far Greater than Rubies

Day 2
Introducing …
The Author of Life

Day 3
Signed, Sealed,
and Delivered

Day 4
Journey with a Purpose

Day 5
Claim Your Prize!

Proverbs 31:10-31 was written as an acrostic, each verse beginning with a successive letter of the Hebrew alphabet. Scholars speculate it was organized for easy memorization and to serve as a guide to aid men in identifying a virtuous woman, a wife of noble character.

Many times well-meaning Christians teach Proverbs 31 and focus more on the woman's domestic qualities than her internal attributes. I recently plugged "Proverbs 31" into my Internet search engine and was amazed at the number of references it identified. Many were home pages containing such things as recipes, gardening tips, sewing patterns, and parenting advice. Some were very enjoyable; others were disturbing.

One Internet site actually claimed that to be a virtuous woman you must cook, clean, sew, garden, and be a stay-at-home mother. Another made the point that you are out of God's will if you wear pants, short hair, or choose a method other than homeschooling to educate your children. If that were true, one, two, three strikes—I'm out! I believe it is stretching biblical instruction to say that all Christian women must make the same choices to be virtuous women in God's eyes.

"*She is worth far more than rubies.*"

Proverbs 31:10

Day 1
Far Greater than Rubies

The Proverbs 31 woman possessed many virtues, yet she almost certainly did not wake up one morning suddenly virtuous. Becoming virtuous is a process. Let us begin our quest to discover what it takes to become a virtuous woman. Proverbs 31:10 states that the virtuous woman is a rare find with "worth far above rubies."

Read Job 28:12-28.
What question begins the passage? (v. 12)

_____

What does verse 18 say is more valuable than rubies? _____

While many of the domestic qualities of the Proverbs 31 woman were standard for her time period and culture, her quality of "fearing the Lord" remains standard for all time.

Psalm 111:10 tells us that, "the fear of the Lord is the beginning of wisdom." Before we can begin to understand the mystery of obtaining wisdom (week 4), we must first explore what it is to fear the Lord, as mentioned in Proverbs 31:30.

"*A woman who fears the Lord is to be praised.*"

Proverbs 31:30

Describe in your own words what you think "fear of the Lord" means.

_____

_____

_____

The Bible mentions several types of fear, so we need to understand the type of fear in the phrase, "fear of the Lord."

Personal Reflection

Where do we get "fear of the Lord"? _____

Who strengthens and encourages believers? (Acts 9:31) _____

Fear of the Lord originates with God and is bestowed through the power of the Holy Spirit. We must know God in a personal way, not to merely know about Him. The first step in knowing God is to place our faith in Jesus Christ, acknowledging Him as the only way to a personal relationship with God.

The only way to the Father is by: (Check one.)

❏ feeding the poor   ❏ raising land-mine victim awareness
❏ getting baptized   ❏ practicing random acts of kindness
❏ being a good person   ❏ your grandparents praying for you
❏ believing in His Son   ❏ attending church

Briefly describe your first encounter with the Author of life.

_____

_____

If you have not personally received Jesus Christ, I plead with you to do so. Pray and ask Christ into your life. Then get counsel from your leader, pastor, or a mature Christian you trust.

Fear and love must coexist in us before we can please and rightly serve God. *New Unger's Bible Dictionary* describes *fear of the Lord* with the phrases that appear below. Circle any of the characteristics in which you are weak.

- dreads God's displeasure _____

- desires God's favor _____

- reveres God's holiness _____

- submits cheerfully to God's will _____

- is grateful for God's benefits _____

- sincerely worships God _____

- conscientiously obeys God's commandments[1] _____

Beside each of the characteristics you circled, write some suggested actions for change. (Example: submits cheerfully to God's will–I will not whine.)

How do we begin to fear the Lord? Is it an inborn instinct? Is this virtue available to everyone or is it only bestowed on a blessed few? The Proverbs 31 woman's ability to "fear the Lord" was key in her being set apart from other women. If we are to become virtuous, we must possess this attribute. We will seek to better understand what it is to fear the Lord in the days to come.

Look back over the characteristics you circled. Pray, asking God to help you develop these attributes so you may revere Him, as He deserves.

"The fear of the Lord— that is wisdom."

Job 28:28

Day 2
Introducing ... The Author of Life

The term "fear of the Lord" is found most often in the Old Testament. It can also be found in the teachings of the New Testament.

We cannot know God apart from faith in His Son, and we cannot fear God if we don't know Him. Jesus said, "I have come that they may have life, and have it to the full" (John 10:10). Fearing the Lord is a critical aspect of having that abundant life.

Hebrews 4:16 encourages us to approach God's throne of grace with confidence, so we may receive mercy and find grace to help us in our time of need. Think of a time you needed grace—maybe you committed a sin so atrocious that you still feel uncomfortable to think about it. Now picture yourself approaching God's throne of grace. You have an appointment with the Kings of kings and Lord of lords. He is waiting for you. You begin to approach the Great Almighty. Do you walk? Do you run? Do you hang your head low and drag your feet? Once there, what do you say?

No doubt, most of us would be filled with awe and reverence (a healthy fear of the Lord) as we approach Him. Would we also come with confidence and total assurance that our God is approachable and will not cast us away? Christians can take comfort in the fact that Jesus is our High Priest, so we can approach the Father with confidence (see Heb. 4:14-16).

Many people today cannot understand how the God who showed wrath and judgment in the Old Testament could love them. At one point, this served as a barrier to my embracing the Christian faith. When I finally gave my life over to Christ, many of my questions remained unanswered, but the love of Christ and His offer of unfailing love was enough to convince me to trust Him to be my Savior. I knew in my heart I would gain a better understanding of the God depicted in the Old Testament. Let's examine some Old Testament teaching about fearing God.

Moses' final words encouraged the Israelites to remember their covenant with God and to pass it to future generations, so that their days would be successful in the promised land. Moses instructed the people to read through the law (the Book of Deuteronomy) every seven years in the hearing of all the people (Deut. 31:9-13).

Read Deuteronomy 31:12. What is the purpose of reading through the law?

_____

Many people forfeit the abundant life for 'just a life.'

Read Deuteronomy 31:13. Who else must hear this law? Why?

_____

I am so grateful for this wonderful promise. We can learn to fear the Lord. I am one of those people who had to learn to fear God.

What is your impression of God as He is depicted in the Old Testament?
- ❏ He had a really short fuse!
- ❏ Never read it. Ignorance is bliss.
- ❏ I thought patience was a virtue.
- ❏ "It's my way or the highway!"
- ❏ Really scaaaaaaaaary!
- ❏ It has never really mattered to me.
- ❏ I'd hate to be on His bad side!
- ❏ Other: _____
- ❏ He was a lot more patient than I would have been.

On days 3 and 4 we will join the Israelites as they take part in the exodus from Egypt. Ask God to prepare your heart as you seek to understand His character in the Old Testament.

Day 3
Signed, Sealed, and Delivered

I am fascinated with the exodus of the Israelite people from Egypt. When properly understood, it becomes a love story second only to the sacrificial death of Christ. God kept His promise to His people when after they had served over 400 years in slavery to the Egyptians, He raised up Moses to deliver them from bondage and into the promised land.

Read Exodus 1:8-14. How did the Egyptians deal with the Israelite people? (Circle all that apply.)

appointed slave masters over them   dealt with them shrewdly
oppressed them with labor   mistreated them ruthlessly
forced them into hard labor   made them work in the fields

Exodus 1:14 says: "They made their lives _____ with hard labor in brick and mortar and with all kinds of work in the fields; in all their hard labor the Egyptians _____ them ruthlessly."

> "Their children, who do not know this law, must hear it and learn to fear the Lord your God as long as you live in the land you are crossing the Jordan to possess."
>
> Deuteronomy 31:13

Put yourself in the Israelites' place. How do you imagine they were feeling?

_____

Complete the following: After years of bondage to the Egyptians, I would have ...

❏ written to my embassy.   ❏ cried myself to sleep at night.

❏ formed a mutiny.   ❏ asked my master for time off.

❏ visited an Egyptian therapist. ❏ cried out to God for deliverance.

Have you ever been used (ruthlessly) for another's personal gain?

_____

How did it feel? _____

_____

Did they view you as a person of worth or as a means to an end?

_____

Most of us are familiar with Moses' life: his discovery in a basket on the river by the Pharaoh's daughter, his adoption into her family, and his witnessing a Hebrew's beating; his killing the Egyptian who had administered the beating, and his flight to Midian where God revealed His plan and appointed Moses to deliver the Israelites from Egypt.

Read Exodus 3:7-17. What caused God to respond to the people? (v. 7)

_____

What is the plan? (v. 8-10)_____

_____

Had God forgotten His people? Did He care about their suffering? (v. 16-17)

_____

This passage portrays a God of: ❑ love. ❑ judgment and wrath.

Why do you think God is concerned with people's suffering today?

_____

Read Exodus 5:1-2,6-14. How did Pharaoh respond to Moses' request to let the Israelite people go to worship their God and offer sacrifices to Him?

_____

_____

We see that God reminded Moses of His promise and predicted Pharaoh's hardness of heart. God sent Moses back with a series of plagues to force Pharaoh to let the people go, to worship God, and offer God sacrifices. God already knew Pharaoh would not allow the people to go until the tenth and final plague. As you read the following summary of the plagues, consider how they demonstrate God's love and sovereignty.

The Plagues

Blood: Egyptians depended on life-sustaining waters of the Nile. Some theologians think turning it into blood was punishment for using it to kill Israelite babies.

Frogs: In Egypt, frogs were the symbol of fertility. How ironic that the Pharaoh had failed in his attempts to limit the population of the Israelites.

Gnats: *Gnats* basically means *lice* or *stinging gnats*. Pharaoh's magicians could not duplicate this plague and advised him that this plague was possibly caused by God. Pharaoh's heart grew harder as God predicted.

Flies: Exclusive to the Egyptians, this plague did not affect the Israelites' land. God made this distinction to show His favor to the Israelite people.

Livestock: This plague was also exclusive to the livestock of the Egyptians; the livestock of the Israelites remained untouched.

Boils: Boils broke out only on the Egyptians and to further spite them, God allowed the magicians to be infected as well.

Hail: God warned Pharaoh through Moses that man and beast would be killed by this storm if they did not bring them in from the field for protection. Exodus 9:20

"Assemble the people—men, women and children, and the aliens living in your towns—so they can listen and learn to fear the Lord your God and follow carefully all the words of this law."

Deuteronomy 31:12

(NKJV) says, "He who feared the word of the Lord among the servants of Pharaoh made his servants and his livestock flee to the houses." In spite of the Egyptians' strong beliefs in gods and goddesses, many were beginning to "fear" the Lord.

Locusts: What little food had grown or been recovered since the hail storm was destroyed by locusts. Scripture says there had never been locusts such as these, nor shall there be in the future.

Darkness: Darkness fell over the land of the Egyptians only; Israelites had light in their dwellings. Where was the Egyptian deity, the sun god Ra, during this plague?

Death: The last plague was the most devastating to the Egyptians and included the death of all the firstborn in the land of Egypt, from the firstborn of Pharaoh to the firstborn of livestock. There was a great cry in the land of Egypt, for there was not a house where there was not one dead.

The Israelites, however, were spared from God's wrath. God had given them specific instructions on how to insure they would be spared losing their firstborn to death. By sacrificing a lamb and putting its blood on the sides and top of their doorposts, the angel of death would know they belonged to the Lord and would pass over them. This is called the Passover. The Israelites were told that the Passover should serve as a day to commemorate and celebrate for generations to come. It serves as a reminder of God's love and mercy in delivering the Israelites out of Egypt.

Because of this last plague, Pharaoh agreed to let the Israelites go. The exodus from Egypt began with an estimated 2,000,000 Israelites leaving Egypt with their livestock, unleavened dough for making bread, and materials handed over by the Egyptians. As predicted by the Lord, they also plundered the Egyptians.

Imagine you are an Israelite As you are leaving Egypt, what are your thoughts toward God?

_____

Do you question His love now? _____

How will the great acts you have witnessed impact both your faith and your children's faith?

_____

_____

Day 4
Journey with a Purpose

We pick up today where the Israelites experienced awe and reverence toward God for the great miracles they had witnessed. The Israelites were just days into their exodus from Egypt when, all of a sudden, they heard the thundering of horse's hooves and looked back to see the Egyptian army coming. The Pharaoh had changed his mind—he had decided to make one last attempt to prevent the Israelites from leaving by hemming them in at the Red Sea.

In addition to witnessing the plagues, the Israelites had the best compass to aid their escape. They were led by God Himself as He sent a pillar of cloud to guide them by day and a pillar of fire to guide them by night. Read Exodus 14:10-12 to discover their response as they exited Egypt and came up to the Red Sea with the Egyptians quickly approaching from behind.

In all honesty, what would your response have been?
- ❏ Tap your slippers together and chant, "There's no place like home."
- ❏ Hold up a "will work for food" sign.
- ❏ Grab the kids, face the Red Sea, and anticipate a miracle from God.
- ❏ Stick up your thumb and appear to be hitchhiking.
- ❏ Get your last will and testament in order.
- ❏ Scream out, "Let 'em have it, Lord!"

God parted the Red Sea when Moses raised his staff. To protect the Israelites from the approaching army, an angel of God withdrew from the front and went behind them. The pillar of cloud also moved behind the Israelites and brought darkness between them and the Egyptians. The waters of the Red Sea rose up on either side so that the Israelites could cross through the Red Sea.

As the Israelites walked through, the Egyptians pursued them. The pillar of cloud threw them into confusion; their chariot wheels fell off. Once the Israelites reached the other side, Moses again raised his staff and the water swept over the Egyptian army. Not one of them survived.

Read Exodus 14:31 to see their new response after witnessing this great miracle. "And when the Israelites saw the great power the Lord displayed against the Egyptians, the people _____ _____ _____ and put their _____ in him and in Moses his servant."

According to this verse, what follows fear of the Lord? _____

What changed their attitude from complaining to reverence and awe?

_____

I find it somewhat amusing that after witnessing so many miracles prior to the exodus, the Israelites suddenly assumed the Great Miracle Maker was on His lunch break. Throughout their journey in the wilderness, the Israelites would witness many more miracles. Unfortunately, the Israelites' awe and reverence of God was always short-lived.

How are we similar to the Israelites in remembering our deliverance?

_____

_____

Again and again, God forgave the Israelites' rebellion at the prompting of His servant Moses. As a result, Moses declared that God is slow to anger, abounding in love, and forgiving of sin and rebellion. However, the Israelite's sin was not without consequences. As a result of their failure to fear the Lord, all of the men 20 years or older (except Caleb and Joshua, who responded in faith) would die in the desert. Only their children would enter the promised land.

Read Numbers 14:24. "Because my servant Caleb has a _____ spirit and follows me _____, I will bring him into the land he went to, and his descendants will inherit it."

The Hebrew word for *spirit* in this verse is *ruwach* (roó-akh). It means breath or sensible (even violent) exhalation. Imagine that! It is sensible to follow the Lord! To commit to Him with a whole heart should become as second nature as breathing. It was this spirit in Caleb that led to his

Do you think it was a coincidence that Moses was spared as a baby, raised among the Egyptians, and appointed by God to deliver the Israelites out of Egypt? Or, is it possible that God planned the birth of Moses for this very purpose?

uncompromising devotion to follow God wholeheartedly. God noticed Caleb's commitment, and Caleb was rewarded because he feared the Lord.

Self check: If you had been among the Israelites who made the exodus from Egypt, would you have been known more for:
❏ your grumbling; or ❏ your fear of the Lord?

Pray and ask God to give you the ability, with the help of the Holy Spirit, to follow Him wholeheartedly in the days to come.

Day 5
Claim Your Prize!

Yesterday we ended by discussing Caleb's commitment to follow God with all of his heart. One can safely assume that this was no easy task, given the fact that out of all of the estimated 600,000 Israelites who were part of the exodus, only Caleb and Joshua were allowed to enter the promised land (Ex. 12:37).

Though it does not come anywhere close to comparison, I still remember the excitement I felt when I was elected as one of six cheerleaders out of over 100 girls trying out in junior high school. No doubt, it had little to do with my character, and more to do with my ability to do back handsprings across the gym floor during tryouts. I will never forget the pure elation I felt when I heard my name called over the public address system. I was chosen. I was something. I was one of a few girls who would get to don that uniform the following year. Are you impressed? I hope not!

Think of a time where you were chosen for something. What were you feeling at that time?

_____

_____

_____

How would it feel to be recognized by God for your whole-hearted devotion to follow Him?

_____

_____

_____

My cheerleader days are long gone, and I have since determined that it is a far greater honor to be noticed by God for my ability to follow Him fully. As Christians, we are all on His squad, but few will be recognized for their whole-hearted devotion to Him. I would like to come to a point in my life where, more often than not, I can lay my head down to rest at night and tell God, "Today I have followed You fully, with all my heart. Nothing hindered me from doing Your will."

Read these verses and circle references to serving God with a whole heart:

"Now, O Israel, what does the Lord your God ask of you but to fear the Lord your God, to walk in all his ways, to love him, to serve the Lord your God with all your heart and with all your soul, and to observe the Lord's commands and decrees that I am giving you today for your own good" (Deut. 10:12-13).

"But be sure to fear the Lord and serve him faithfully with all your heart; consider what great things he has done for you" (1 Sam. 12:24).

"He gave them these orders: 'You must serve faithfully and wholeheartedly in the fear of the Lord' " (2 Chron. 19:9).

Read Proverbs 2:1-6 and summarize it below in your own words.

_____

_____

Scripture abounds with benefits to those who fear the Lord. A few examples include God's promise to provide for, protect, reveal Himself to, save, and

love those who fear Him. Read at least five of the Scriptures below. In the margin note benefits promised to those who fear God.

Psalms 25:14; 33:18; 34:7,9; 85:9; 103:11,13; 103:17-18; 111:5,10; 115:11,13; 118:4; 128:1; 145:19; 147:11

Proverbs 1:7; 9:10; 10:27; 14:27; 15:33; 19:23; 22:4

Isaiah 33:6; Luke 1:50

Which of the verses above had the greatest impact on you? Circle them. After reading the verses, do you better understand the type of devotion the Proverbs 31 woman had for her God?

I am deeply troubled by the number of people, Christians included, who have little fear of the Lord. Most people never give God the time of day. Few will recognize Him as the very Creator of life, and the few who do will never take the time to say thank you. The majority will pay homage to those who impress the world with their talents and skills, while ignoring the handiwork of God all around them. We are no different today from the Israelite people who quickly forgot God's covenant and pledge of unfailing love and turned their hearts to idols. God desires our whole heart. The Proverbs 31 woman followed God with a whole-hearted devotion. If we desire to be virtuous women, we must be willing to do the same.

Review the third type of ground covered last week on day 5. How do "cares of the world" and the "deceitfulness of wealth" hinder people today from whole-hearted commitment to God?

_____

What things keep you from following God with whole-hearted devotion?

_____

What do you need to change to become a woman who fears the Lord?

_____

What's your plan for making these changes?

[1] *New Ungers Bible Dictionary, Revised Edition* (Chicago, IL., Moody Press, 1988) 404.

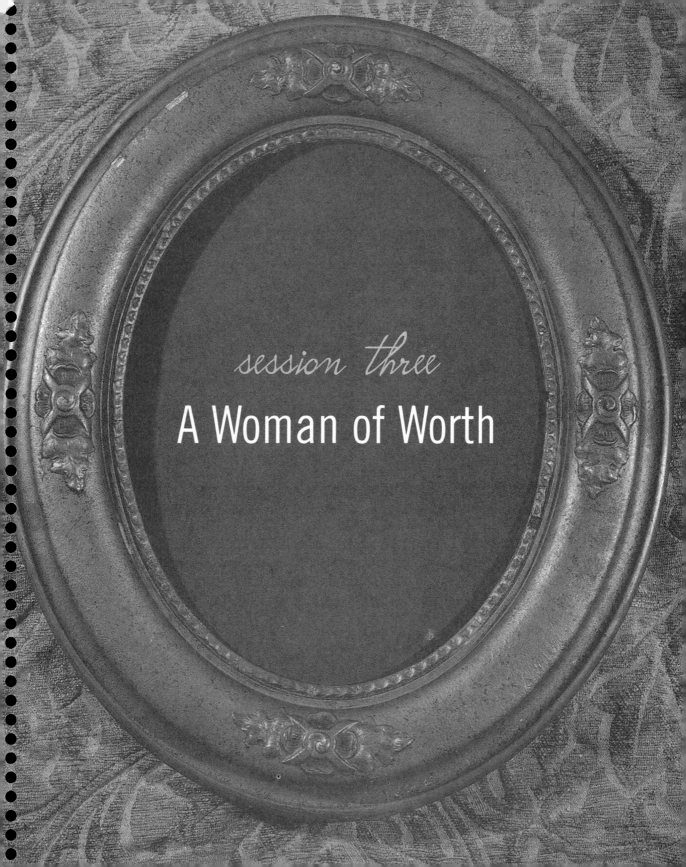

session *three*

A Woman of Worth

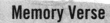
The Virtuous Woman

Memory Verse

"Do not conform any longer to the pattern of this world, but be transformed by the renewing of your mind. Then you will be able to test and approve what God's will is— his good, pleasing and perfect will."

Romans 12:2

This Week's Lessons

Day 1
Your Worth
According to the World

Day 2
Your Worth
According to God

Day 3
What Brings You
to the Well?

Day 4
Prepare for Battle

Day 5
What Keeps You
from the Well?

I'll never forget her face as she handed me a folded-up piece of paper. She could not speak. She came to the front in need of prayer at the end of a women's event. As I stood face-to-face with her, my heart broke. Her eyes were hollow and distant, as if she had given up long ago. Her face was stained with tears and her hand was shaking uncontrollably as she handed me the slip of paper. Whatever was written on it obviously caused her too much shame to be able to speak it aloud as a prayer request.

I unfolded the paper and read, "God can never forgive me—I killed my unborn baby by doing crack cocaine." I looked up to find her staring at the ground, unable to even make eye contact with me. She had covered her face with her hands; her body was shivering as she silently sobbed. I wrapped my arms around this precious woman and said, "You've come to the right place. I have good news for you."

She had been a Christian for years, yet she had been unable to understand God's message of forgiveness. Somehow she had imagined it was possible to reach a point where her sin could outweigh God's ability to forgive. I don't know where she is today, but when she left that day, her face radiated with the freedom only Christ can grant. She came lacking self-worth and left with her worth redefined. Only God can do that. I know that firsthand, because He did the same thing for me.

What secret ingredient did the Proverbs 31 woman possess that gave her so much confidence? What kept her from conforming to the patterns of the world? At the very core of her life was her relationship with God. Her "worth" was not far above rubies because of her beauty, knowledge, or achievements. Her worth was established in her Maker, and she recognized her value in Him. Will her secret work for women today?

day 1

Your Worth According to the World

As you stand in the supermarket check-out line, a fashion magazine catches your eye with the subtitle "Lust Lessons." Or how about "Six Quick Steps to a Sexy Stomach" or "Flirting Online." Maybe you see "What Men Think About Your Look" or even "Get a Better Body–For Sex." These are actual articles that have run in popular fashion magazines. *The New York Times,* April 4, 1999, carried an article entitled "Women's magazines flip past feminism–Magazine defends sex advice as part of feminism." Gloria Steinem, a long-time and vocal feminist, attacks fashion magazine editors for offering "sexual advice about pleasing men as part of a larger movement toward making women feel bad about themselves."

The irony is that most of the fashion magazines have editors who consider themselves feminists. Bonnie Fuller, editor-in-chief for *Glamour*, defends *Glamour's* many sex articles by pointing out that sexual advice is a product of the women's movement. She further claims, "it would be unempowering for women not to be able to read about sex as much as they wanted."

Let's get this straight: the women's movement, which loathes dependency on men, has now become a movement that encourages women to look for ways to please men sexually. How ironic that to feel "empowered," women are now dependent on men! It amazes me that women's-movement leaders honestly feel their efforts build women's self-worth. Is it any wonder women are so confused when it comes to defining their worth?

In your opinion, why do most of the forces of media refuse to offer material that encourages the pursuit of virtuous qualities among women?

_____

How frightening that the self-worth of so many women has been molded by worldly influences! In spite of the fact that we live in the information era and are bombarded with messages to aid us in the pursuit of self-worth, women have never been more empty and confused.

Without looking it up, how do you define self-worth?

_____

Which of the following would boost your self-worth?

- ❏ losing weight
- ❏ toning up
- ❏ clear skin
- ❏ facial beauty
- ❏ a thriving social life
- ❏ a successful career
- ❏ receiving compliments
- ❏ plastic surgery
- ❏ dressing fashionably
- ❏ driving an expensive car
- ❏ making a decent income
- ❏ getting married
- ❏ having well-behaved children
- ❏ having children who succeed
- ❏ a very nice home
- ❏ leading a Bible study
- ❏ having a husband who makes a decent income
- ❏ being recognized as a really awesome Christian
- ❏ being recognized as a leader in my church

Believe it or not, none of these should influence self-worth. God never intended for our worth to be built on anything other than our standing in His Son. If our worth is based on what we do, what we look like, or what others think of us, we will be guilty of "conforming to the pattern of this world," as mentioned in Romans 12:2. I battle daily the temptation to base my worth on the world's influences. Certainly nothing is wrong with looking our best and being good stewards of our talents and abilities; the danger comes when our worth becomes dependent on these factors.

On which of the following should our worth be based?

- ❏ What others think of us
- ❏ What we look like
- ❏ How God views us
- ❏ Our talents and abilities
- ❏ A little of each one

As we end today, look back over the items you may have checked in the chart that you felt would lend to your self-worth. Pray and ask God to prepare your heart to receive His truth regarding your base of self-worth.

day 2
Your Worth According to God

Imagine standing in the check-out line and seeing magazines with the featured articles, "How Does God See You?" or "What God Thinks About Your Look." How about "Improve Your Body–It's the Temple of God"?

Would most women buy those magazines? ❑ Yes ❑ No Why or why not?

_____

Would you buy: ❑ the above magazines or ❑ fashion magazines?

I believe God desires a new women's movement–women who base their worth on God alone. For this movement to begin, Christian women must quit playing the world's games of defining worth. Why believe the world's lies when we have access to a loving, perfect Heavenly Father who has our best interests in mind? Surely the God who created us also has a plan for us. He makes no profit on the advice given in the pages of His Word, and His definition of worth does not fluctuate with the changing times.

The Proverbs 31 woman had worth "far above rubies" because of who she was in God's eyes, not because of her achievements. Our worth should be based exclusively on who we are in Christ. To base our worth on anything else is building our foundation on shifting sand. When the rains come (and they will), a foundation built by the blueprints of the world will not stand. Psalm 33:11 says, "The plans of the Lord stand firm forever, the purposes of his heart through all generations." Somewhere along the line, the chain of mistruth will have to be broken. Perhaps it will start with you.

How do we hand down to our children the world's equations for worth?

_____

_____

God desires a new women's movement.

41

Personal Reflection

Imagine you are assigned to write the article, "How Does God See You?" Using the following verses, write a statement for each that would build support for your article:

Psalm 139:14:

_____

John 1:12:

_____

John 15:15:

_____

1 Corinthians 3:16:

_____

2 Corinthians 5:21:

_____

Proverbs 31:29 says, "Many women do noble things, but you surpass them all." My dictionary defines *noble* as "notable, excellent, magnificent, of a superior nature."

Name several women who have been praised for doing noble things:

_____

List some noble things you have done.

_____

Do you desire to be a woman who is known more for her noble deeds or a woman who fears the Lord?

_____

Look back at the verses that supported the article, "How Does God See You?" Which one meant the most to you? Why? Close in prayer and ask God to help you base your worth on His standard and not the world's.

day 3
What Brings You to the Well?

The more I speak to women's groups, the more convinced I am that the majority of women (including Christians) have misdefined their worth. Somewhere along the way they missed the boat when it comes to basing their worth in Jesus Christ. Let's use our remaining time together this week to cover two common factors that hinder women from defining their worth in Christ and keep them from experiencing abundant life in Christ.

The first hindrance to defining worth in Jesus Christ is guilt that stems from an inability or refusal to accept God's forgiveness. One of the best illustrations of Jesus' restoring worth to a woman burdened by guilt is His encounter with the Samaritan woman at the well.

Read John 4:7-30. When Jesus asked the Samaritan woman for a drink, she responded with …
- ❑ anger. She was a part of the women's movement in Samaria.
- ❑ silence. Her parents taught her never to talk to strangers.
- ❑ shock. Jews did not associate with Samaritans.

Interesting facts:
- Most Jews avoided taking the route through Samaria back to Galilee because of their deep prejudice against Samaritans. In verse 4, John stated Jesus "had" or "needed" to go through Samaria. This word may signal that Jesus knew in advance of a ministry need in Samaria.
- The prejudices of the Jews against Samaritans went back over 500 years.
- There was water in the village of Sychar where the Samaritan woman lived. It is not clear why she traveled to a well outside her village, but some theologians speculate it could have been a result of the ostracism she felt in her village for her misdeeds.
- Rabbis avoided contact with women in public.
- Men did not normally speak to women, even close relatives, in public.
- The disciples were not present at the well. If they had been, the Samaritan woman may not have spoken.

Jesus crossed ❑ no ❑ two ❑ many boundaries to speak to this woman.

Do you think Jesus was at the well by coincidence when the Samaritan woman arrived, or did He know in advance she was coming? Assuming Jesus set up this divine appointment with the Samaritan woman, what hope does this give women who are burdened by sin?

_____

In verses 10-14, Jesus explained "Living Water." What is Jesus' distinction between the water in the well and Living Water?

_____

In verse 15, the woman was extremely curious and asked Jesus to give her Living Water. At that point, He told her to go, call her husband, and come back. She then told Him that she had no husband.

Jesus addressed the fact that she had no husband. Further, He pointed out that she had had five husbands and that the man she was currently with was not her husband. If He already knew this, why did He bother to ask her to call her husband before He would give her Living Water?

❑ He wanted her to understand that He was more than a mere man sitting at a well.

❑ It was necessary to address her sin before she could receive Living Water.

❑ By bringing awareness to her sin, He was able to show her how desperately she needed Living Water.

❑ All of the above.

The woman then speculated that He was a prophet. When she said that the coming Messiah would explain all things, Jesus declared:

❑ "Let me know if you see him."   ❑ "I who speak to you am he."

❑ "Don't believe everything you hear."

In verses 28-30, she left her water jar, returned to her town, and told the people of her encounter. As a result, they made their way to see Jesus. Many of the Samaritans from that town believed in Him because of the woman's testimony: "He told me everything I ever did" (John 4:39). The Samaritan woman had a lasting impact for generations to come.

As women, every one of us can relate to the Samaritan woman. I have been this woman and so have you. Though we may not have committed her same sins, we have all had reason to go to the well for Living Water. A failure to admit the need for Living Water is the result of pride.

List what might bring you to the well. Be general rather than graphic. Include anything that has caused you guilt or shame.

_____

_____

Does anything you listed still plague you today? ❑ Yes ❑ No

Close by praying and sharing openly with God about the things you listed. Ask Him to apply His Living Water to any current areas of sin.

"Whoever drinks the water I give him will never thirst. Indeed, the water I give him will become in him a spring of water welling up to eternal life."

John 4:14

day 4
Prepare for Battle

Imagine the Samaritan woman responding to Jesus' offer of Living Water with, "Thanks, but I just can't take it. My sin is far too great." As absurd as it sounds, many of us have done just that when it comes to God's forgiveness. We may still be hanging out at the well, burdened by the same shame and condemnation that brought us in the first place. Some of us may have received Living Water, yet have failed to recognize the power it possesses.

Read John 7:37-39. Whom does Jesus invite to come and drink? (v. 37)

_____

What will flow from within the person who believes in Jesus? (v. 38)

_____

Living Water refers to … (v. 39)

_____

Do you believe a person can receive the Holy Spirit but fail to depend on His power? ❏ Yes ❏ No

How might this hinder women from leaving the well?

_____

Have you received Living Water? ❏ Yes ❏ No
Have you left the well? ❏ Yes ❏ No
Have you had opportunity to share Living Water with others? ❏ Yes ❏ No

How comforting that Jesus did not scream at the woman about her sin. He focused on her need before He addressed behavior. If Christians followed Christ's example when addressing those in sin, many would line up to enter churches to hear more about Living Water. Jesus never made His offer of Living Water contingent upon changed behavior, nor should we.

How might we learn from the way Jesus addressed the Samaritan woman?

_____

If Jesus' offer of Living Water covers sin and shame, we must wonder why so many Christian women are still stuck at the well, unable to put the past in its place. Could it be the work of the enemy?

Does it make sense that Satan desires as many women as possible to be hung up at the well of forgiveness, burdened with sin and shame?
❏ Yes ❏ No ❏ Not sure

How does it serve Satan if women stay at the well?

_____

Satan would like nothing more than to render women ineffective as believers in Jesus Christ. We must recognize him for who he really is. Christian women who are burdened with shame and guilt are of no worry to him. He knows that if he can keep them at the well, doubting God's love and forgiveness, they will have little impact in furthering the kingdom of God. Think about it. If you are not completely free from your past, how can you race from the well with excitement to share with others this wonderful gift?

Your pursuit to become a virtuous woman will be in vain if you fail to accept and appreciate God's forgiveness. If this is particularly critical in your life, here are some Scriptures to meditate on: Psalm 103:12; Romans 4:7-8; 8:1; Hebrews 10:17.

I used to think it would be a luxury to forget my past sins. However, I have come to the conclusion that the purpose of our remembering past sin is to remind us of what Christ has done for us. It should leave us feeling overwhelmed with gratitude rather than feeling condemned . Once the truth behind the cross begins to set in, you will never be the same. When Jesus carried to the cross the burden of our sin, He cried out, "It is finished." Can you accept that it is finished?

> "Many of
> the Samaritans
> from that town
> believed in him
> because of the
> woman's testimony,
> 'He told me
> everything
> I ever did.' "
>
> John 4:39

Look at your list of things that have brought you to the well (day 3). Draw a cross over the list and write, "It is finished" as a banner over the top.

The Samaritan woman impacted Samaria for generations to come because she was faithful to receive Living Water, consume (experience) Living Water, leave the well, and share Living Water with others. Will your faithfulness impact future generations in the same way?

No sin is too great for the Living Water of Jesus Christ. To remain at the well is sin. What an insult to refuse our Lord's offer! Jesus took our sin to the cross in exchange for Living Water. He bore our sin and chose to die that we might live. When the magnitude of the cross sinks in, we are forever changed. Our worth is redefined. The world pales in the shadow of the cross. Our hearts are grateful because no one else ever loved us like that.

day 5
What Keeps You from the Well?

After I spoke on temptation at a women's event, a woman approached me. She had been a Christian for many years. She and her husband were very involved in their local church, and she taught Sunday School. They were committed to raising their four children in the church and to teaching them Christian principles. Then she dropped the bomb. She was having an affair with a coworker. It had been going on for over two years and at times she would end it, only to resume it days later. She spoke confidently of her salvation and was more than knowledgeable when it came to God's forgiveness. She said she knew what she was doing was wrong, yet she seemed unwilling to give it up. She said that this man truly loved her and that he complimented her more than her husband. She did not believe that obedience to Jesus Christ is more fulfilling than any earthly pleasure.

Many Christian women are enticed by the world and give in to its desires. If we do not fully embrace the message of the cross, only time separates us from returning to the familiar and comfortable. Dying to sin and self is not a one-time event. It must be a daily (or for me, moment-by-moment) exercise. Some Christians choose "feeling good" over "doing good."

My youngest son, Hayden, has a knack for catching lizards. He took one to his kindergarten class show-and-tell. When he got home, I encouraged him to let it go free because it wasn't looking well. He and his visiting classmate went outside to grant the lizard freedom. Shortly they came back with a flat rock and a permanent marker. (A permanent marker in the hands of a five-year-old will get a mother's attention.) They explained that they had buried the lizard. The rock was to be the tombstone. Before helping them with spelling the lizard's epitaph, I asked Hayden if the lizard had actually died. He responded very matter-of-factly, "Mom, he was almost dead." The story has a happy ending. We rescued the poor lizard in time. He raced off, and I doubt he will return to our house anytime soon.

It occurs to me that quite a few "almost-dead" Christians populate the world. Many attend Bible studies and serve in ministry leadership positions. They are knowledgeable about prayer and quiet times; they fill church pews. They are "almost dead" because they have given up just about every-thing to follow Jesus Christ. Yet certain sins still master them occasionally, causing their relationship with God to be less abundant and full. By refus-ing to completely die daily to sin in their life, they miss the abundant life Christ intends. I speak from experience; I used to be an almost-dead Christian. If I'm not careful, I could be one again.

I think almost-dead Christians are the world's most miserable people because they've tasted abundant life. They know deep in their heart no earthly pleasure can compare to a deeper relationship with Jesus Christ.

Have you ever been an "almost-dead Christian?" ❏ Yes ❏ No

I believe Satan works on "almost-dead" Christians by trying to keep them in bondage to the world's pleasures. One can only imagine the number of Christians with tremendous potential who have given over to the "feel-good" message of the world rather than the "do-good" message of God. Ironically, nothing feels as good as choosing God's ways over the ways of the world.

Can you think of a time when you were able to choose God over the world in a tempting situation? ❏ Yes ❏ No If so, how did it feel?

Many times we make excuses for our sinfulness. Mark any excuses below you may have been guilty of saying or believing in the past.

- ❏ "I didn't know better."
- ❏ "It felt so right."
- ❏ "It was harmless."
- ❏ "I'm a victim."
- ❏ "I'm not perfect."
- ❏ "That's not like me."
- ❏ "I was caught off guard."

- ❏ "I'm not ready to grow up yet."
- ❏ "I fell into the wrong crowd."
- ❏ "I have low self-esteem."
- ❏ "I'm at a rough place in my life."
- ❏ "Don't I deserve a little happiness."
- ❏ "I didn't plan for this to happen."
- ❏ "At least I didn't do what she did."

As long as we are in the habit of making excuses, we will be unable to die to sin. Many rationalize and minimize their sin, but as long as we fail to die to sin, we will forfeit the opportunity to have a deep and meaningful relationship with Jesus Christ. When we grow callous to sin, we minimize the sacrifice Jesus made on the cross. We've all had reason to visit the well. Isaiah 64:6 reminds us that our most righteous deeds are as filthy rags to God. The truth is, we are all worthless. A virtuous woman will recognize that her worth is all a gift from the grace of God. If we have not been forever changed by the Living Water offered by Jesus Christ, we missed something at the well. If an overwhelming sense of gratitude to Christ is not present in your life, is it possible that your pride hinders you from experiencing true worth?

Pride, like all other sin, is reason enough to visit the well. Whether we have terminated a pregnancy by doing crack cocaine, had an affair, or experienced a case of pride, we are no different from the Samaritan woman. Each of us has reason to visit the well. Each of us is in desperate need of Living Water. With one drink of Living Water, we will take on a new identity. We become holy and blameless in God's sight. When He looks at us, He sees in us the righteousness of Jesus Christ. If that isn't a life-changing thought, I don't know what is. True self-worth is found at the well of forgiveness.

The choice is yours:
Worth according to the world: Worth = What you look like.
Worth = What you do.
Worth = What others think of you.
OR
Worth according to God: Worth = Who you are in Christ.

session four

A Woman of Wisdom

Memory Verse

"For wisdom is more precious than rubies, and

nothing you desire can compare with her."

Proverbs 8:11

This Week's Lessons

Day 1
A Picture of
Godly Wisdom

Day 2
Wisdom According
to the World

Day 3
A Priceless Treasure

Day 4
Yours for the Asking

Day 5
She Speaks with Wisdom

I'll never forget the first time I heard the name Ada Ferguson. My friend and pastor's wife, Carolyn, had been invited to be a part of a small group meeting weekly in Ada's kitchen. For weeks, Carolyn went on and on about Ada Ferguson and the godly wisdom she possessed. Finally I could stand it no longer. I asked to join the group. I mean, why not? I could certainly use a little wisdom in my life. Prior to the first meeting, I was a little apprehensive and not sure what to expect. I pictured an elderly woman with gray hair swept up in a bun, reading Scripture aloud from a big King James Bible, emphasizing the thee's and thou's.

Nothing could prepare me for the first meeting. When she answered the door, she was nothing like my image of a woman of wisdom. She was beautiful, stylish, and had a haircut to die for. She didn't seem old enough to possess wisdom. She immediately put me at ease and we all gathered around her kitchen table with coffee in hand. She prayed with ease and comfort, as if she was accustomed to spending many hours at the throne. She spoke to the Father with reverence, praising Him for our husbands and our responsibility as mothers to raise our children as godly seed for the next generation.

It quickly became clear that Ada Ferguson knew God's Word backwards, forwards, sideways, and upside down. Whether we were talking about husbands, kids, politics, decorating, or mothers-in-law, Ada always seemed to have morsels of truth from God's Word. She could take the Scriptures and make them come alive. Her comments were always spoken with confident authority, laced with wisdom, and shared in a spirit of humility. She was not puffed up with knowledge of Scripture, but desperately dependent on walking with Christ on a daily basis. She was sensitive to sin in her life and would grieve over missed opportunities to share the love of Christ or for her children's friends who did not know the Lord. She spoke with compassion for everyone instead of speaking with harsh judgment. What made Ada so wise? Did she inherit some sort of wisdom gene? Is it possible for just anyone to obtain the kind of godly wisdom Ada possesses?

day 1
A Picture of Godly Wisdom

When I discovered the Proverbs 31 passage, I thought to be a virtuous woman you had to tip the scale with homemaking skills. Ada possessed many homemaking skills, but at the center of her life was her relationship with Christ. Ada did not possess wisdom as a result of being a good house-keeper or prioritizing her husband and children, but as a result of knowing God. The depth of her relationship with the Savior defined her role as wife, mother, friend, and mentor. Ada looked forward to time alone with God and got up early in the morning to meet with Him. She also looked for ways to please her husband and children, and to be a support to them. Her countenance reflected that she lived a fulfilling and abundant life.

Ada shared that, though she had been a Christian for many years, she did not really understand what it meant to make Christ the Lord of her life until her oldest child was two years old. At the time, Ada's husband was not a Christian, and she adopted 1 Peter 3:1-6 as her life verses. She was committed to winning her husband to faith in Jesus Christ without preach-ing or nagging. Several years ago, Ada's faithfulness was rewarded and her husband walked forward on a Sunday morning and gave his life to Christ. God drew him that morning, but Ada's commitment 29 years prior played a large part in his name being added to the Book of Life. God honored Ada's faithful obedience and her pursuit of godly wisdom. Today Ada and her husband minister together in their local church.

Ada continues to have an impact on my life. I call her often just to run situations past her and to gain her wisdom and insight. Many people would share advice or personal opinion, but Ada is always faithful to share pearls of godly wisdom and point me in the direction of the Savior.

Have you ever known anyone like Ada? ☒ Yes ❑ No

How has this person influenced your life? _help w/ childre_

decisions on discipline

> *"Wives, in the same way be submissive to your husbands so that, if any of them do not believe the word, they may be won over without words by the behavior of their wives, when they see the purity and reverence of your lives."*
>
> 1 Peter 3:1-2

> *"Then they can train the younger women to love their husbands and children, to be self-controlled and pure, to be busy at home, to be kind, and to be subject to their husbands, so that no one will malign the word of God."*
>
> Titus 2:4-5

Ada is wise because: (T or F)

____ She majored in philosophy.

_✓_ She prioritizes spending time alone with God.

_✓_ She emulates the domestic skills of the Proverbs 31 woman.

_✓_ She commits Scripture to memory.

____ She reads fiction novels.

_✓_ Her life centers around her relationship with Jesus Christ.

____ God showed favor to her among women.

_✓_ She finds answers to life's questions in God's Word.

____ She has obtained much knowledge of Socrates, Aristotle, and Plato.

____ She reads the newspaper and watches the news daily.

____ She has a master's degree.

_✓_ She prioritizes prayer.

____ She was voted "most likely to be wise" in high school.

Do you currently look up to an older woman? ❑ Yes ❑✓No

If so, what about her demonstrates wisdom? _____

_____

Do you have a mentor in your life who models Titus 2:3-5? ❑✓Yes ❑ No

Have you considered mentoring a younger woman? ❑ Yes ❑✓No

Share your thoughts on how developing a relationship with a godly mentor might help you in the quest for wisdom.

Someone to share your heart w/ & won't judge you

_____

As you end today's study, pray and ask God to show you the value of godly wisdom this week.

day 2

Wisdom According to the World

Before we attempt to acquire the godly virtue of wisdom, we must first make a distinction between wisdom and knowledge. Knowledge is a body of information: facts and figures. Wisdom, on the other hand, is good judgment: knowing what to do with knowledge.

In week 1 we discovered the importance of possessing knowledge to live up to the world's definition of the ideal woman. From the moment we are born, we begin to store up knowledge. In school the goal is to obtain as much knowledge as possible. We are applauded for good report cards, honors classes, honor roll, and graduating at the top of our class. When we get to college, honor students are a dime a dozen and the challenge to excel is even greater.

My husband, Keith, possesses great knowledge. He graduated first in his college class in chemical engineering and received many honors for academic achievements. One of his greatest honors came when he was chosen as one of 50 students out of approximately 50,000 to receive a Presidential Scholarship. As part of the selection process, Keith and the other candidates had to go before a panel consisting of the dean of each college at the University of Texas. Each of the deans asked a challenging question to gauge knowledge of each student. The process was grueling and intimidating with the deans seated in a semi-circle facing each student.

One of the deans asked Keith, "To what do you attribute your knowledge?" Keith responded, "My knowledge is a gift from God and without Him it would be worthless." He went on to share his testimony and emphasized that his faith in Christ was far more important than knowledge. As the deans stared back with shock and disapproval, Keith thought, "I just blew a scholarship." However, on the way back to his dorm, he practically skipped with joy, having testified to the truth. To this day, Keith believes God gave him the scholarship because of his faithfulness in answering the question. My husband is gifted with knowledge, but more importantly, he is gifted with wisdom.

Personal Reflection

In your opinion, what is the difference between godly wisdom and worldly knowledge?

G- seeks God - W- educational

Is it possible for just anyone to possess godly wisdom? _yes,_
if you seek it.

Read James 1:5. What must one do to acquire wisdom? _ask God_

When you pray, are you in the habit of asking God for His wisdom?

not always, I should more

Read the following verses and jot down how wisdom can be obtained.

Ecclesiastes. 2:26 _God gives_

Isaiah 33:6 _Fear of Lord_

1 Corinthians 12:8 _Spirit_

Colossians 1:9 _prayer_

According to the verses you just read, the best way to obtain wisdom is to:

- ❏ Watch "Oprah."
- ☑ Look to God.
- ❏ Rely on the Holy Spirit.
- ❏ Fear the Lord.
- ☑ Seek to live a life pleasing to God.
- ❏ Ask a philosophy major.
- ❏ Give Ada or Keith a call.
- ❏ Ask your mother–she knows everything.

Knowledge the world emphasizes is very different than the type of knowledge God's Word emphasizes. Look up the following verses pertaining to knowledge. Write below to what the word *knowledge* refers in each verse.

2 Corinthians 4:6 _gospel message_

1 Timothy 2:3-4 _salvation_

Titus 1:1-2 _truthfulness_

Hebrews 10:26 _truth_

2 Peter 1:2-3 _know God_

2 Peter 3:18 _know God_

What kind of knowledge does God value?

- ❏ how to clone human beings
- ❏ $\pi = 3.14159$
- ❏ truth of the gospel message
- ❏ the latest scoop–"inquiring minds want to know"
- ☑ truth that leads to godliness, resting on the hope of eternal life
- ❏ glory of God in the face of Christ
- ❏ creating a space station on Mars
- ☑ our Lord and Savior Jesus Christ

Obviously, knowledge is not a bad thing as long as it is partnered with wisdom and used responsibly. It is far easier to gain knowledge alone, than to obtain both wisdom and knowledge.

In the pursuit to become a virtuous woman, we need to obtain both wisdom and knowledge from the Holy One. Wisdom is the quality that makes the virtuous woman a rare find with worth far above rubies. Many women will possess knowledge, but only few will possess wisdom. The world may esteem the pursuit of knowledge, but God honors the pursuit of godly wisdom.

"*Blessed is the man who finds wisdom, the man who gains understanding.*"

Proverbs 3:13

day 3
A Priceless Treasure

Throughout the Bible, wisdom is often compared to gold, silver, or precious stones. The Book of Proverbs says "wisdom is more precious than rubies, and nothing you desire can compare with her" (8:11). It says to get wisdom is much better than to get gold (16:16).

Read Job 28:15-19. Why do you think Job considered wisdom to be of such great worth?

can't put value on it

I still remember my first jewelry box. It was white with pink flowers. When you opened the lid, it would play music and a ballerina would twirl around. My love of jewelry started when I was a little girl. I would feed quarters into the gumball machine at the grocery store until I was rewarded with a jewelry trinket. As I got older, it didn't take long for me to figure out the difference between a cubic zirconium and a real diamond.

Never did I imagine, however, that I would someday be up to my ears in diamonds. Now before you jump to any conclusions, let me explain. From the time I graduated from college, I have run a diamond business out of my home. I have accounts with diamond brokers across the country. They mail me diamonds to show to my customers. If any of the diamonds don't sell, I mail them right back. Since I have no storefront or inventory, I can sell under retail to my customers. As a result, my little home-based business quickly turned into a thriving jewelry operation.

When it comes to diamonds and fine jewelry, I have seen it all. I mail back packages of diamonds to brokers insured for ten's of thousands of dollars. My kids think it is perfectly natural to sell diamonds across the kitchen table. When my youngest child was four years old, he had a friend over to play while I was showing diamonds to a customer. When his friend asked what I was doing, he said, "Selling diamonds—doesn't your mom sell diamonds?" I have seen so many diamonds over the years. What's amazing, however, is the more diamonds I saw, the less I wanted them for myself. (My husband will tell you that having the business was worth that revelation alone.)

Why the change in my desires? The more diamonds I saw, the less valuable they seemed. They weren't that rare to me. If I had a party to attend, I could borrow an extravagant piece from one of my brokers and be on my way. I could adorn myself with valuable jewels without ever owning them!

This would not be possible, of course, regarding wisdom. Wisdom cannot be bought, reproduced in synthetic form, or borrowed for an evening. It is far more valuable than any jewelry trinket money can buy, yet not many women say, "Wisdom is a girl's best friend." Most women expend more energy pursuing the worlds' valuables than seeking the precious treasure of wisdom offered by God.

The best thing about wisdom is that it's free to those who ask, and it has a lasting impact for generations to come. The virtuous woman has worth far above rubies because she has chosen to adorn herself with wisdom rather than rubies.

What would be your most prized possession from your jewelry box?

wedding ring / pearls - Tere

To whom will you hand it down someday? *girls + son*

What is the significance behind the above piece? *given by Joe - took sacrifice to have*

What can you do to see that when others look back on your life they will say you valued wisdom over the baubles contained in your jewelry box?

hope not

day 4
Yours for the Asking

> "I pray that you, being rooted and established in love, may have power, together with all the saints, to grasp how wide and long and high and deep is the love of Christ, and to know this love that surpasses knowledge—that you may be filled to the measure of all the fullness of God."
>
> Ephesians 3:17-19

Fortunately, wisdom is not available only to a few, but can be possessed by anyone. However, as Eve, and I, learned the hard way, there are no short-cuts to obtaining wisdom. Early in my marriage Keith and I were looking to purchase a house. We prayed and asked God to give us wisdom to make the right decision. Shortly thereafter, we found a house we liked, but it had escalating mortgage payments. Keith saw red flags all over the deal, while I saw vaulted ceilings and a master bathtub big enough to swim laps in. I allowed my feelings to take over and convinced my sweet husband that God led us to the house. (Hmmm. Do I recall Eve pulling the same stunt?) The house became a painful lesson with high price. Fortunately, we were able to sell the house two years later. Because of that experience, we exercised better judgment buying our next house.

I made the mistake of treating wisdom like an item in a vending machine. Just put your quarter in and out it comes. James 1:5 says that if we lack wisdom, just ask and God will give it liberally, right? Of course, I made the mistake of assuming that God will answer according to my time constraints and my feelings. True wisdom develops over time and comes as a result of walking with God on a regular basis. In a nutshell, godly wisdom is "think-ing like God." We cannot think like God unless we know Him by walking with Him on a regular basis.

If you are like me, share an experience when you prayed for wisdom but instead made the decision based on your human emotion and feelings.

Car _____

_____

How might wisdom "save you" in the sense described in Proverbs 2:12?

deliver you _____

In the margin list the things wisdom will do for you (Prov. 4:6-9).

Which of these three proverbs most impacts your thinking about wisdom, and why? (Prov. 9:12; 12:8; (24:14))

_____

How might wisdom change a person's appearance? (Eccl. 8:1)

shine w/ wisdom

What one attribute most indicates wisdom? (Jas. 3:13)

good conversation

Describe a situation in which you exercised godly wisdom:

kept my mouth shut when I want to be unkind!

Take an internal check. In what areas do you need improvement?

negative

Many Scriptures contrast *wisdom* and *folly*. Read the following verses and underline what folly is associated with:

"Folly is loud … undisciplined and without knowledge" (Prov. 9:13).
"Folly entices others to sin" (Prov. 9:14-18).
"The mouth of a fool invites ruin" (Prov. 10:14).
"Whoever spreads slander (gossip) is a fool" (Prov. 10:18).
✗ "Where words are many, sin is not absent" (Prov. 10:19).
"The folly of fools is deception" (Prov. 14:8).
"A fool's eyes wander to the ends of the earth" (Prov. 17:24).
"He who trusts in himself is a fool" (Prov. 28:26).

End today by praying and asking God to place a desire on your heart to be in continual pursuit of wisdom.

(margin notes)
- *preserve*
- *keep*
- *understand*
- *promote*
- *hona*
- *grace + glory*

day 5
She Speaks with Wisdom

Proverbs 31:26 says, "She speaks with wisdom, and faithful instruction is on her tongue." In week 2, we saw that fearing the Lord is the key quality of a virtuous woman. The Proverbs 31 woman spoke with wisdom—one of the by-products of fearing the Lord. One of the best examples in Scripture of a woman who "spoke with wisdom" is Abigail. Ironically, Abigail was married to Nabal, whose name means "fool" or "wicked." The story of Abigail and Nabal is a wonderful example of the contrast between wisdom and folly. As you read the passage, keep in mind the attributes of wisdom and folly listed in day 4.

Read 1 Samuel 25:2-42.

David was a fugitive from Saul. Word of David's strength had gotten out and many, including Abigail, speculated the Lord would someday appoint him leader over Israel. While in hiding from Saul, David settled in the Desert of Maon, and eventually found himself and his followers in need of food and provisions. David sent ten of his men to Nabal, a wealthy man living nearby, to solicit provisions. David's men had provided protection to Nabal's shepherds from plunderers robbing the threshing floors. The customs of the day dictated that Nabal assist David.

When David's men arrived and made the request for provisions to Nabal, how did he respond? (1 Sam. 25:10-11)

_____

Not only did Nabal refuse to send provisions, he also attacked David's character. How did David respond when his men return empty-handed and with news of the character attack Nabal launched on him? (1 Sam. 25:13)

_____

_____

At this point, how do you suppose David felt?
❑ very under appreciated, having provided protection for Nabal
❑ angry that his character had been assaulted
❑ like a "nobody" in the eyes of Nabal
❑ all of the above

Abigail entered the picture when one of the servants told her the story of Nabal's refusal to help David. The servant told Abigail of the protection David and his men had provided them in the past. What did he say about Nabal in 1 Samuel 25:17?

_____

How did Abigail respond to the servant's report? (Choose two.)
❑ She shared frustration over the many needy people who attempt to take advantage of their wealth.
❑ She loaded a large stock of provisions on donkeys.
❑ She shooed them off, more concerned with what to wear to the sheep-shearing party that evening.
❑ She sent her servants ahead with provisions, followed behind, and did not tell Nabal.

What was David planning to do to Nabal? (v. 21-22)

_____

Abigail humbly bowed before David and appealed to him. She complemented David and assured him of God's faithfulness to someday appoint him leader over Israel. What were her motives in doing this?

❑ She had been influenced by the articles in the fashion magazines that encourage women to be pleasing to men.
❑ She was trying to make Nabal jealous.
❑ She was an intelligent, God-fearing woman.
❑ Her best friend told her to leave Nabal for David because he was destined to be king someday.
❑ She was hoping to protect her household from David's wrath.
❑ She was looking for a way out of an unhappy marriage.

> *The virtuous woman is more interested in clothing herself with wisdom than fine jewels. Truly, wisdom is a girl's best friend.*

What was the first thing David said to her after her appeal? (v. 32)

_____

In verses 33-34 David blessed Abigail for her good judgment and for keeping him from bloodshed. David granted Abigail's request and sent her home in peace. I'm sure Abigail was experiencing a mixed bag of feelings on her way home. She must have felt tremendous relief having spared her household from death, yet great sadness in having to return to a man as wicked as Nabal. Moreover, she was likely feeling somewhat fearful at the thought of sharing her whereabouts with Nabal.

In your opinion, did Abigail speak words of wisdom and faithful instruction to David? ❏ Yes ❏ No

Use your imagination. If Abigail was a woman of folly, what do you think she would have said?

_____

_____

How might you have handled this situation?

_____

When she returned: (T or F)
_____ Nabal was cowering in a corner with fear, having heard from a servant that David was on his way to kill him.
_____ Nabal was raging mad with jealousy.
_____ Nabal was absolutely clueless as to what had just occurred.
_____ Nabal was bragging to his friends about his statues and great wealth.
_____ Nabal had had a bit too much to drink.
_____ Nabal had worried himself sick looking for Abigail.
_____ Nabal was holding a banquet like a king.

Abigail once again, used good judgment and waited until morning when Nabal was sober to tell him of the harm that almost came to his household. We do not know exactly what she said, but Scripture indicates she told him "all these things." It was then that his heart failed and he became like a stone. Ten days later, the Lord struck (smote) Nabal and he died.

Once again, contrast Abigail to a woman of folly in this situation. What might a woman of folly said or done?

_____

_____

When David heard the news of Nabal's death, he praised the Lord for upholding his cause against Nabal and for bringing Nabal's wrongdoing down on his own head. He then sent his servants to Abigail, with the purpose of asking her to become his wife. Abigail, still true to her character, bowed down with her face to the ground and said, "Here is your maidservant, ready to serve you and wash the feet of my master's servants." Keep in mind that wealth was no stranger to Abigail, yet she humbly gave herself to David.

Abigail is a wonderful example of someone who possessed much more than knowledge. Her testimony offers women the hope that in spite of negative circumstances, they can still become a women of wisdom. Abigail's wisdom enabled her to endure an unhappy marriage when many would have become bitter. Not many women today could match Abigail's integrity. Most women faced with her situation would have bailed out a long time ago at the bidding of family, friends, and most marriage counselors. What a testimony in a time where divorces are a dime a dozen over "incompatibility" issues. The irony is that many in the world would call Abigail the "fool" for remaining in a bad marriage. Some may even applaud Nabal's aggressive business tactics and ability to accumulate wealth. Fortunately, Abigail was not in the habit of looking to the world for guidance. She was utterly dependent on God for her future and happiness, and as always, God rewarded her commitment to Him.

As you close this week, pray, asking God in faith, according to James 1:5, to give you wisdom. Ask Him to make it the desire of your heart in your pursuit to become a woman who "surpasses them all."

> *"She speaks with wisdom, and faithful instruction is on her tongue."*
>
> Proverbs 31:26

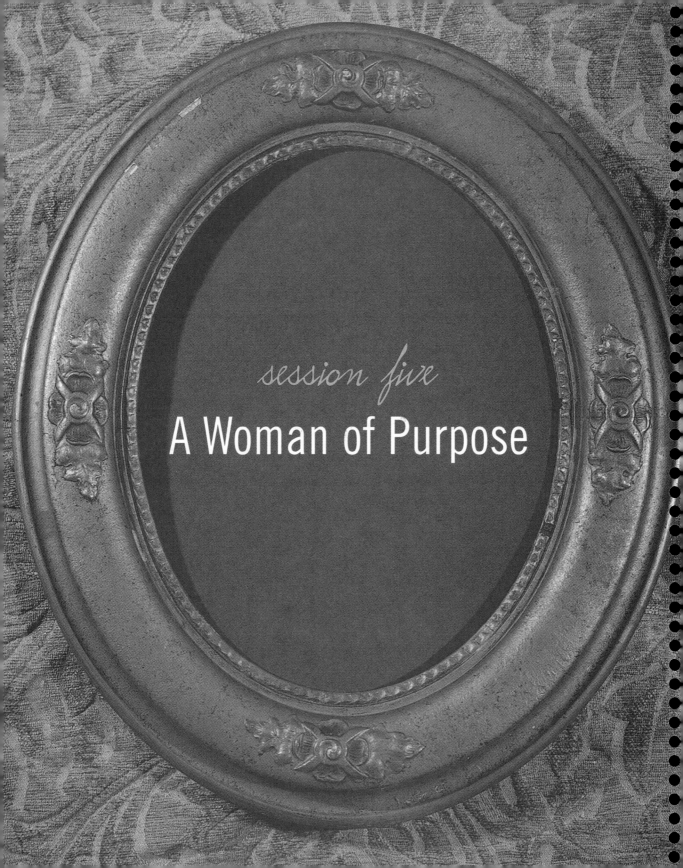

session five

A Woman of Purpose

"Then he said to his disciples, "The harvest is plentiful but the workers are few. Ask the Lord of the harvest, therefore, to send out workers into his harvest field."

Matthew 9:37-38

Memory Verse

This Week's Lessons

Day 1
Why Are We Here?

Day 2
What Is Our Job?

Day 3
A Place in the Harvest

Day 4
A Wife of Noble Character

Day 5
Her Children Arise and
Call Her Blessed

When Keith and I were first married, he quickly established a five-year plan to organize our lives. The plan called for me to work full-time for several years before starting our family. This "plan" would enable us to save money for a house and get our feet on the ground financially.

The plan worked great for four months until I discovered I was expecting a child. I'll never forget the morning I took the pregnancy test. Keith was out on the porch having his quiet time, no doubt pleading with God for the results to be negative. When I read the positive result on the test, I couldn't mask my elation and set out to share the good news. Even though I knew a baby wasn't part of the "plan," I somehow imagined that Keith, too, would be overjoyed with the news. When I stepped out on the porch and shared that I was in fact pregnant, his first words were, "You can't be pregnant. We don't have a baby in the budget." A dozen roses later, all was forgiven and we adjusted to the new plan. Twelve years later, we can't imagine life without our Ryan.

Can God interrupt our lives at any time and throw us off of our carefully plotted courses? You bet! We are so accustomed to plotting and planning our lives that we naturally assume God will follow closely behind, sprinkling magic fairy dust on our man-made plans. When it comes to finding purpose in life, imagine that the very God of heaven wants to be the God of our day-planners, as well! Will our day-planners match up with His, when it comes to finding purpose in life? Are we about the business He assigned us?

The Proverbs 31 woman was a woman of purpose because she prioritized her God above all else in her life. A virtuous woman will allow God to dictate her purpose, rather than look to the world for guidance. Though the circumstances of our lives may change, our God-given purpose will remain steadfast for all times.

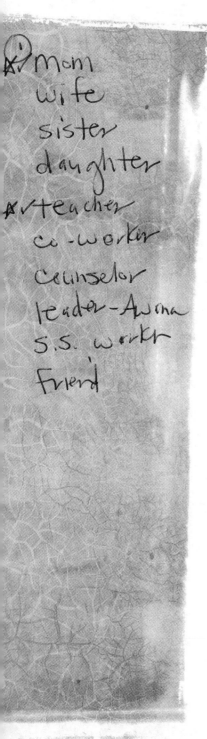

day 1
Why Are We Here?

Finding purpose is a common quest in life. The result can lead to an abundant life or a life of misery. No doubt, the Proverbs 31 woman was a woman of purpose. She wore many different hats. Throughout our lives we, too, will wear many different hats. Some of them might include: daughter, sister, friend, mother, wife, coworker, grandmother, aunt, servant, homeroom mother, neighbor, Sunday School teacher, and CEO of a major corporation. One can easily become overwhelmed when looking for purpose in each role. The good news is that if we focus on our ultimate God-given purpose, success will come, regardless of the hats we wear.

Read through Proverbs 31:10-31. List the many hats the woman wore:

wife, cook, farmer, seamstrist, sells clothes, counselor, mother

In the margin list some of the hats you currently wear.

Place a check beside the roles that require the majority of your time and a star beside those that bring you the greatest sense of purpose.

What do you think is your greatest purpose in being placed on earth?

telling others about God

What does Revelation 4:11 suggest about your purpose?

God's pleasure

The *New Living Translation* reads, "For you created everything, and it is for your pleasure that they exist and were created." The Greek word for *pleasure* is *thelema*, which translates into desire, pleasure, and will.[1]

The margin notes read:
mom
wife
sister
daughter
teacher
co-worker
counselor
leader—Awana
S.S. worker
friend

What an awesome thought that the God of the universe created us for His pleasure. I can't help but wonder if He ever regrets His decision. The majority of people today don't even acknowledge Him, much less seek to please Him. Most will go through their lives without recognizing Him, let alone giving Him the reverence He deserves. Our purpose in this life is to bring glory, honor, and pleasure to our Maker in everything we do.

The verse appears again in the margin. Mark through the words *they* and *were* and replace them with *I* and *was*. Now read the edited verse aloud. Think about it and say it again, if necessary. Do you believe it?

Think about how you spend your days. Consult your calendar or refrigerator door, if that is helpful. List some tangible ways you can better use your time, bring God pleasure, and acknowledge Him as the God of your time:

others first, less selfish

One of my favorite passages is Psalm 73:25-26. The NLT says, "Whom have I in heaven but you? I desire you more than anything on earth. My health may fail, and my spirit may grow weak, but God remains the strength of my heart; he is mine forever."

I have committed this verse to memory and I repeat it to myself often. The part that first caught my eye was, "I desire you more than anything on earth." At that time I was an "almost-dead Christian," playing the game, but failing to "walk the talk." When I read the verse, I could not honestly say, "I desire you more than anything on earth." I began to pray and ask God to help me in the pursuit to make Him the number-one desire of my heart. I can now say that I desire God more than anything on earth. He is my everything. My purpose in life is to honor, worship, and revere Him in everything I do.

Pray aloud and tell God, "I want to desire You more than anything." Only pray this if it is truly the desire of your heart. Include everything–your husband, children, hobbies, church activities, job, material possessions, strongholds, addictions, areas of sin–everything. Thank God for creating you for His pleasure. May that truth take root as you pray.

"For you created everything, and it is for your pleasure that ~~they~~ *I* exist and ~~were~~ *was* created."

Revelation 4:11, NLT

day 2
What Is Our Job?

Jesus was about to make His last appearance before He ascended to be with the Father. Any time during His three-year ministry Christ could have given the disciples their assignment, but He knew the best use of their time was to sit and to learn from Him firsthand. He knew that if the disciples really got to know Him, they would be ready for their ultimate assignment.

Read Matthew 28:18-20. What task did Jesus give the disciples?

Great Commission

When the time came for Jesus to give final marching orders, the disciples knew who He was. They loved Him more than life itself. Their devotion was so strong they eventually died carrying out their assignments.

We must imitate Jesus' strategy. Both we and those we disciple must get to know and love Him more than life itself. Then we will find it natural to desire to make Him known. Sometimes we are so concerned with recruiting others that we fail to encourage them to get to know Him.

How does a Christian learn to love Christ more than life?

Seek Him

Several years ago I joined a health club. I was determined to follow through with my new exercise plan. At first I went all the time, and within months I was in pretty good shape. Then my life got busy and the first thing to go was the health club.

As Christians, it is not enough to "join the club." We must be willing to take the advice and direction of the trainers and implement it on a regular basis, or we will not see progress. Once we begin the pursuit to know Christ, He will equip us for the task of making Him known to others.

Describe your workout plan to get to know Christ:

Devotion at night, prayer in/before school.

When I became a Christian I had a tremendous burden to get the good news of God's love out to others. Then I went through "my apathetic years." During those years, I often found myself mad at God. I had joined the club and served Him fervently in my initial years, so what happened? I attended church, read my Bible off and on, and prayed, but that "kumbaya/campfire" feeling was gone. God had called me as a speaker several years prior, so I was even speaking to groups during that time. As I look back, I realize I spoke from a head knowledge of Scripture. In my misery, I began to pray and specifically ask God to spark revival in my heart.

Little did I know that for revival I would have to walk the painful path of coming to the end of myself. I had to hand the reigns of control over to God. Why do we fear that giving God absolute control of our lives will end up in our living in a thatched hut, teaching macrame to village children?

I finally realized that I needed God. I realized how weak I was on my own. I finally committed to the workout plan and began to prioritize my time with the Trainer. The more I continued the workout, the stronger I became. It was during this process that I began to grasp the depth of His love like never before. As a result, I couldn't help but return His love and encourage others.

Have you come to the realization that you desperately need Jesus Christ–not just to give you a home in heaven, but to help you live? ☑ Yes ❑ No

Read Luke 10:38-42. This passage is not a favorite among women. It evokes immediate guilt. I relate more to Martha, but Jesus' answer always pierces my heart. "Martha, Martha, you are worried and bothered about so many things ... Mary has chosen the good part."

I wonder how Martha responded: "OK, Lord, I guess that means we settle for paper plates and takeout tonight." We Marthas think: "Who will take care of things if we don't?" The truth is, Jesus would tell us to "chill out" if the details became a replacement for our time with Him.

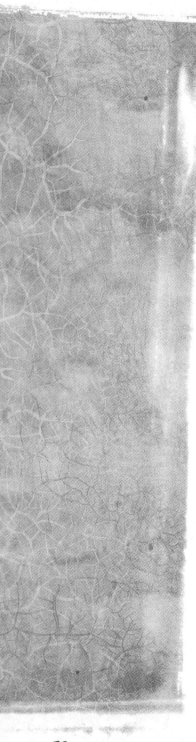

Sometimes we imagine that to become Proverbs 31 women, we must become a sort of Bible-toting Martha Stewart. You can only trudge so long without the much-needed fuel of time alone with God on a daily basis. I was once more concerned with the work of the Lord than the Lord of the work.

Do you more resemble: ☑ Martha or ❑ Mary?

Just as with any workout, no shortcuts exist for getting in shape. Consistent and persistent discipline to stick to the workout will show results. Unless you prioritize prayer, reading, worship, and meditating on His Word, it will be impossible to become a virtuous woman. The good news is that it's never too late to start the workout. What an awesome God we serve.

Close in prayer, asking God to help you in your new workout plan.

day 3
A Place in the Harvest

Part two of the kingdom agenda is to "make Him known." After we develop the habit of "knowing Him," we are ready to take our places in the harvest. If we follow Him, God will be faithful to place us in a harvest where our individual gifts and talents can be used for His glory.

I learned this the hard way as a new believer when I signed up to help with the meals ministry at my church. Let's just say that it was a mismatch from day one. Sometimes we are so anxious to serve God that we jump the gun and run ahead of Him, taking a wrong turn along the way.

Once we are assigned to a harvest, what is our job?

_do it_

Read 2 Corinthians 5:18-21. What ministry have we been given? (v. 18)

reconcile

Wow, what an awesome job we have! Did you know that you were called to the ministry of reconciliation? Did you catch your job title? Ambassador. Not just any ambassador, but Christ's ambassador! An ambassador is a representative. God has chosen each of us to represent Jesus Christ.

We need a burden for each harvest we encounter. Sometimes God calls us to pray. Other times He shows us we are the answer to that prayer. The harvest can range from our neighborhood to the far corners of the globe.

Describe the harvest(s) in which you currently work:

teacher- many kids don't know Christ!

What harvest most burdens your heart? _my students_

To know God and make Him known is our primary purpose in life. The kingdom agenda should be at the very core of our lives. Everything else, job, marriage, kids, activities, friends, and so forth … is fluff. It's easy to get carried away with other roles and mistakenly assume they are our "primary" purpose in life. Our goal should be to bring glory to God in everything we do, whether our harvest is a neighborhood party or a distant land. We don't have to have a platform in the public eye to make a difference. God is constantly at work, setting up divine appointments and expecting us to share the good news of the kingdom.

In the margin list ways you can make a difference in your everyday life as an ambassador of Christ.

*treat students by being an example of God
*show my kids God's love

Pray and ask God to burden your heart for the lost. If you struggle with sharing your faith, ask Him to strengthen you for the task and to show you your assigned harvest. Ask Him to help you see the lost as "sheep without a Shepherd."

What an awesome privilege to introduce someone to the Good Shepherd. A woman of purpose knows God, and makes Him known to others. A virtuous woman recognizes that the kingdom agenda is her God-given purpose in life.

Personal Reflection

To whom are we are called to minister? _lost_

In Matthew 9:36-38, what reference does Jesus make to the crowd?

Who is the Shepherd? _Jesus_

Are you looking for "sheep without a Shepherd?" ☑ Yes ☐ No

Do you have compassion for them, as Jesus did? ☑ Yes ☐ No

The compassion Jesus showed to the crowd is convicting to me. I really struggle with being critical of people who speak harshly against Christianity. I have to constantly remind myself that they are, "sheep without a Shepherd." How quickly I forget that I, too, used to be a "sheep without a Shepherd."

In Matthew 9:37, Jesus told His disciples about the harvest:

What is the "harvest" to which He referred? _lost_

Are there enough workers? _NO_

In Matthew 9:38, what were the disciples told? _pray_

Do you pray the Lord of the harvest to send workers? ☑ Yes ☑ No

Days 4 and 5 address a woman's purpose as a wife and/or mother. There is no way to discuss the Proverbs 31 woman without addressing the hats she wore as a wife and a mother. Even if these roles are not part of your life, let me encourage you to take a look at days 4 and 5. You never know when God may use you to serve as an encouragement to someone else.

day 4
A Wife of Noble Character

June Cleaver step aside. Here comes the Proverbs 31 woman, known for her virtuosity as a noble wife. She probably has an hourglass figure to boot. Let me remind you that the Proverbs 31 passage was written as a guide for men on what made up the perfect wife. You know, the modern-day equivalent of *How to Snag an Awesome Wife 101*. Let me also warn you that by the end of today, we will all feel guilty. I feel guilty already, and we just started.

In practical terms, interpret the following verses from Proverbs 31.

"Her husband has full confidence in her and lacks nothing of value." (v. 11)

proud of her, know what she can accomplish + do

I couldn't help but wonder if "lacks nothing of value" includes:
an occasional meal loaded with fat grams;
keeping up with the wash so he doesn't run out of dress socks;
being sure he knows exactly where the remote control is at all times; and
trading in the oversized cotton T-shirts we wear at bedtime.

Seriously though, most of us know what would bring our husbands confidence and meet their needs.

What can you do to earn your husband's confidence?

believe in him, trust him

What does your husband value?

#

What can you do to ensure that he lacks nothing of value?

handle household well

"She brings him good, not harm, all the days of her life" (Prov. 31:12).

positive comments

Once again I couldn't help but snicker when I read this one. I instantly thought of my cooking….

How do you bring your husband "good and not harm"?

If you struggled with theses answers, ask your husband what brings him confidence and value. Plan time to talk with him.

"She speaks with wisdom, and faithful instruction is on her tongue." (v. 26)

I try but need more practice

This definitely rules out our three inborn traits as women: whining, nagging, and manipulation; but unless we are willing to give these up, it will be impossible to become the virtuous women God desires us to be. Can you honestly say that you are in the habit of speaking with wisdom and faithful instruction? ❑ Yes ❑ No ☑ Would you believe sometimes?

"She watches over the affairs of her household and does not eat the bread of idleness" (Prov. 31:27).

puts family 1st

I hate that verse, not to mention the one about her candle not going out at night. No doubt, she was a coffee-drinker.

What can you do this week to improve the affairs of your household?

get more organized, keep peace

What are some areas of "idleness" you may need to give up?

T.V.

"Her children arise and call her blessed; her husband also, and he praises her: 'Many women do noble things, but you surpass them all.' "(v. 28-29)

I definitely like that verse. I think if we can succeed in fulfilling the previous verses, it just may be possible! Just recently, my six-year-old son, Hayden, crawled up in my lap and said, "Mom, you are my kinda woman." He didn't exactly call me blessed, but it sure warmed my heart!

Read Titus 2:3-4 to discover how God exhorts older women to encourage wives and mothers. What does it specifically say the older women should train the younger women to do?

❏ Fight to be liberated and burn their bras in the streets.
☑ Love their husbands and children.
❏ Be busy at home.
❏ Wear the pants in the family.
❏ Be subject to their husbands.
❏ Join Helen Reddy in a chorus of "I am Woman, Hear Me Roar."

It is a bit sad and a bit amusing that women have to be trained to love husbands and children. At first it seems absurd until we remember times when our husbands and children have been less than very lovable.

How might an older godly woman (mentor) aid you in the pursuit to be a better wife?

Keep me on track, even when love doesn't seemed deserved

Diane or Doris

If you do not have a mentor, think of someone who might qualify. Jot possible names in the margin.

Having an older, godly woman in my life as a mentor has been invaluable to me. It is nice to know that my mentor, Ada, is just a phone call away when I have a question or concern. I often wonder how many marriages could be saved if women would recognize the need to have an older godly woman to help guide them through the difficulties of marriage.

What we have covered today can be overwhelming. Please persevere. If you are married, close by asking God to help you in your pursuit to become a godly wife. Ask Him to show you how your marriage can be improved. If you are not married, ask Him how you can apply these principles in your life and relationships.

day 5
Her Children Arise and Call Her Blessed

In my early meetings with Ada, I remember her talking often of the importance of finding joy in all we do. She made it clear that our joy must come from our love of Christ and our willingness to serve Him. Because I had not yet defined my worth solely in Christ, I attempted to follow God's standard, but in my own strength. I thought of Ada's advice, "Whatever you do, work at it with all your heart, as working for the Lord, not for men" (Col. 3:23). When my kids spilled juice on my newly-mopped floor, I would try singing "The Joy of the Lord is my Strength" over and over to brainwash myself while cleaning up the mess. It usually worked until they dumped cereal on the floor before I finished cleaning up the juice. By that point my joy had taken a hike–dragging the song with it. The Proverbs 31 woman modeled that the joy of the Lord was her strength, and she didn't just sing about it, she lived it.

No doubt, the most character-building job I have ever had has been as a mother. It has also been my most rewarding. My little munchkins can take me to untold heights of joy, and minutes later, evoke my fleshly nature quicker than someone cutting me off on the freeway. When it comes to parenting advice, I am certainly not an authority. Any good that has come from my parenting skills is by the grace of God. I absolutely cannot do justice to the topic of parenting, but I can highlight some key verses in Proverbs 31 that shed light on the Proverbs 31 woman's parenting.

Read the following verses that pertain to her role as a mother:

Verse 15 (OK, I know what you're thinking … if we had servant girls to help us, we might get up early too, right?)

Verse 21 (Did I just hear an excuse to SHOP?)

Verse 26 (You mean she is not in the habit of screaming, "GET YOUR SHOES ON AND GET IN THE CAR—WE'RE RUNNING LATE!!!")

Verse 27 (She probably didn't watch a lot of soaps.)

Verse 28a (My middle-school child definitely thinks it's not cool to do this— I want to know her secret.)

We cannot study the Proverbs 31 woman without addressing her commitment to family. I do not care to tackle the career/family conflict and receive hate mail for the rest of my life. However, when reading Proverbs 31, one thing is clear: this woman prioritized God and her family above all else.

Whether a woman works in an outside job full-time or stays home full-time, we can still put other things above the priority of God and/or family. Many women work because they prioritize material goods or fear that being a stay-at-home mom lacks challenge and fulfillment. On the other hand, many women stay home with their children full-time and prioritize a neat, well-kept home, or a list of social, or church activities above the needs of their children. Regardless of your situation, the most important thing is to be in the habit of checking in with God and asking Him what works best for your family. Every situation is different, but fortunately none are out of the reach of God's guidance and control.

The most convicting verse to me is Proverbs 31:27, "She watches over the affairs of her household." The Proverbs 31 woman knew what was going on in her household. She was responsible for the physical needs of those in the home, and she was in tune to their emotional needs, as well. She was the facilitator of relationships. She was the emotional heartbeat of the home and the stabilizing factor for her husband and children. We know that she was no sluggard. We know that she spoke with wisdom and instruction. We know she laughed at the days to come. OK, OK, so we hate her, right? How can we measure up to "Little Mrs. Perfect" when it comes to being a mother? We can start by being sure we know what is going on in our household. The Proverbs 31 woman would most likely have known if her children were making metal shrapnel in the garage!

Get to know your children. Talk to them. Spend time with them. Play with them. Laugh with them. Weep with them. Pray with them. Have fun with them. Tell them often that you value them for who they are and not what they do. Apologize to them when you blow it. Love your husband and speak highly of him. But most importantly, let your children witness that the most important thing in your life is Jesus Christ. A mother's greatest calling is to pass on to her children the value of a deep and intimate relationship with Jesus Christ.

Reflect back on days 1-3. How can we impart to our children the call to be ambassadors for Christ?

Be an example

_____

How are you passing down to your children a legacy of true purpose?

_____

_____

_____

End today by reading the statement in the margin. Pray and ask God to equip you to leave this priceless legacy to your children. Share openly with Him anything else He may have laid on your heart.

> *A mother's greatest calling is to pass on to her children the value of a deep and intimate relationship with Jesus Christ.*

---

[1] Spiros Zodhiates et al., eds., *The Complete Word Study Dictionary: New Testament* (Chattanooga, TN: AMG Publishers, 1992).

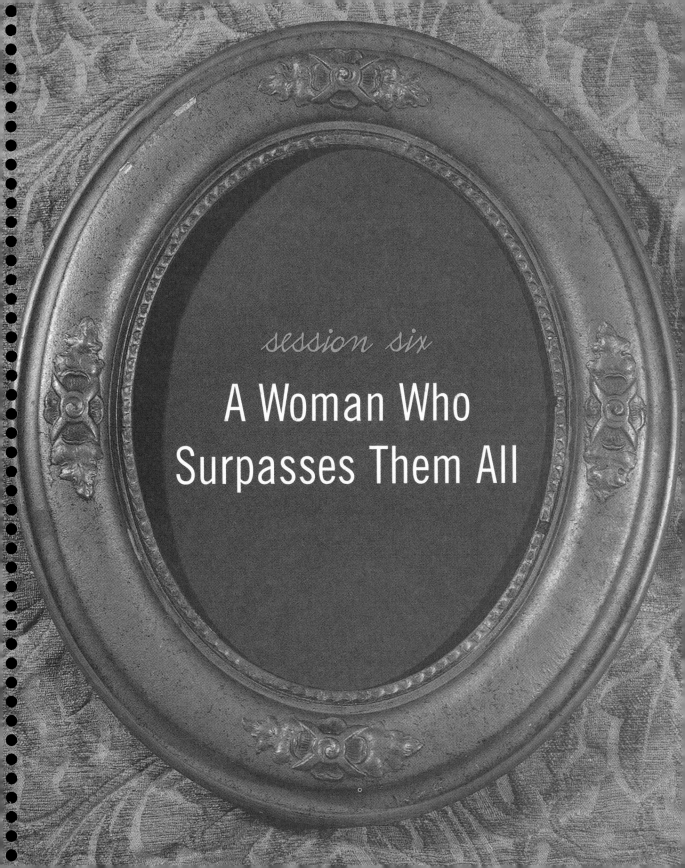

session six

A Woman Who Surpasses Them All

Memory Verse

"Many women do noble things, but you surpass them all.

Charm is deceptive, and beauty is fleeting; but

a woman who fears the Lord is to be praised.

Give her the reward she has earned, and

let her works bring her praise at the city gate."

Proverbs 31:29-31

This Week's Lessons

Can you believe we are on the last week? Are you feeling "virtuous" yet? Have you resigned as SuperWoman and turned in your cape? I hope so! As we end this study, we will cover four more attributes or key qualities of the Proverbs 31 woman, if she wasn't already virtuous enough as a woman who fears the Lord, a woman of worth, a woman of wisdom, and a woman of purpose!

Writing this study has been humbling. In my years in women's ministry, I have met so many godly women who have "virtuous" written all over them. It's hard not to compare myself to them. I am often tempted to become frustrated over the whole pursuit. It reminds me of the refrigerator magnet: "Be patient–He's not finished with me yet." I am always comforted when I read Paul's encouragement to the Christians at Philippi, "He [(God)] who began a good work in you will carry it on to completion until the day of Christ Jesus" (Phil. 1:6). How promising that God is constantly refining us to be more like His Son. If you are feeling overwhelmed with the pursuit to be a virtuous woman, hide that truth in your heart.

day 1

No Time to Waste

I have tried everything. In my attempt to get organized, I have purchased giant wall calendars, memo recorders, Day-Timers, and even highlighted my hair for the blonde excuse. I start off driven by a newfound commitment to bring order to my life, but days later, I am back to scribbling notes on napkins, only to misplace them and spend hours trying to find them. Today we discuss the Proverbs 31 woman's attribute of efficiency. I tried to justify leaving it out, but efficiency appears to be the theme of about one-third of the passage. Unfortunately, we will have to take a look at it.

Read Proverbs 31:13-18. I'm thinking she didn't use the napkin method of organization. I can't help but wonder: didn't she ever just sit and stare into space. What does "not eat the bread of idleness" (v. 27) mean? No more coffee with friends at Starbucks or tuning in with my family to "Jeopardy"? What's the balance?

What did Paul say to do to win others' respect? (1 Thess. 4:11-12)

Comfort + edify

Paul warned the Thessalonians against idle time. Apparently, it had become a problem and people were not "minding their own business," but instead, interfering in the lives of others.

Now read 2 Thessalonians 3:7-13. Second Thessalonians was written about six months later. Had the problem of idleness ❑ improved or ☑ worsened?

What reason did Paul gave for toiling and laboring so hard? (v. 9)

be an example

What was Paul's rule? (v. 10) _no work, no eat_

To what does idleness often lead? (v. 11) _busybodies_

Have you noticed that when we have nothing to do the devil usually finds us something to do? How might misspent idle time hinder women in the pursuit to become virtuous?

gossip, stay focused on God

Perhaps the Proverbs 31 woman abhorred idleness because she feared the consequences it might produce in her own life or maybe, she had witnessed it in the lives of others. Verse 15 also caught my eye: "she provides food for her family and portions for her servant girls." Along with the servants' daily shares of food, she also gave them their tasks for the day. She knew the value of delegating work to others, so as to maximize her time and fulfill the task given.

Many of us do not have the "problem" of delegating chores to hired help, but we have all been in situations where we needed to delegate. Learning to delegate is part of being efficient with our time and energy. At the time it may seem like it's easier to do it all ourselves, but our attitudes and weary spirits prove otherwise in the end.

Can you recall a situation in which you failed to delegate and suffered consequences? ☑ Yes ☐ No If so, identify it briefly.

felt stressed, forget TO DO'S

We could assume that to follow the Proverbs 31 woman's pattern we would have to forgo all leisure and social time. As with most things, balance is key when planning our days. We know that God exhorts us to rest and modeled it Himself when He created the world and rested on the seventh day. We also recall the Mary-and-Martha incident and Jesus' commendation of Mary's ability to sit at His feet. Jesus modeled the need at times to put work aside and get off by Himself, or even fellowship with others.

Part of becoming a virtuous woman is learning the difference between rest, fellowship, and idle time. The Proverbs 31 woman modeled that the best remedy for idleness is to be an efficient and diligent worker.

day 2

Seeds of Selflessness

I wonder if the Proverbs 31 woman ever muttered that familiar cliche´, "We gave at the office." Somehow I doubt it. Proverbs 31:20 says, "She opens her arms to the poor and extends her hands to the needy." If we want to be virtuous women, does that mean we must support every needy cause?

You may be surprised at the intended meaning of *poor* and *needy* in the Proverbs 31 passage. The Hebrew word for *poor* is `*aniy* (aw-nee'), meaning "depressed, in mind or circumstances." The Hebrew word for *needy* is *'ebyown* (eb-yone'), which means "a sense of want, destitute." A modern-day definition would be "beggar" or "poor man." When you include, "depressed, in mind or circumstances," the "poor and needy" category gets bigger. Most of us will not have to look far when reaching out to someone who is needy. Many around us are physically, emotionally, and spiritually poor.

We absolutely can't effectively minister to every needy person who crosses our path. The key will be finding balance when ministering to the needs of others. When someone I know is "emotionally needy," I have a tendency to want to fix the problem. This endeavor can be very time consuming and emotionally draining, not to mention a detriment to my own family. Caretaking can backfire if the one in need begins to depend on us and as a result, is hindered from seeing God at work through the situation.

God does not want us to place on our shoulders the burdens of the needy— that is His job. Often our job is to help them take the next step—providing a meal, an empathetic and listening ear, or encouragement to meet with the pastor or a professional counselor, depending on the situation.

Do you become overly involved in meeting others' needs? ☑ Yes ☐ No
What are some specific ways to find balance in this area?

_____

Just as many "over-give" to the needy, some give for the wrong reasons.

Personal Reflection

Describe a time when you "extended your hand" to someone physically poor or needy.

Bought lunch

Describe a time when you "opened your arms" to someone emotionally poor or needy.

Kelly - listened to her

Describe a time when you assisted someone spiritually poor or needy.

Shauna - scripture vers after "let go"

To which of the three categories of people do you find it easier to minister?

emotionally

Have you ever fallen into any of the categories above? ☑ Yes ☐ No

Which one(s)? emotional + spiritual

Did someone minister to your "neediness" at that time? ☑ Yes ☐ No

How? Toni - listened + gave advice.

Read 1 Corinthians 13:3. What is the essential quality when giving?

charity

What is gained if we lack this quality when giving? *nothing*

To whom did the prophet Ezekiel compare those who have hardened their hearts to the poor and needy? (Ezek. 16:49)

Sodom

What three things contributed to Sodom's insensitivity?

pride, fulness of bread, idleness

Is this still prevalent in our culture today? ☐ Yes ☐ No

Christians are not exempt from the sin of selfishness. While we can't make others help the needy, we must model a giving spirit. Proverbs 14:21 says, "He who despises his neighbor sins, but blessed is he who is kind to the needy." Giving to those in need is certainly one of life's great blessings.

day 3
Tomorrow's Another Day

My kids love to play the "trust/fall" game, in which I stand behind them and they fall backwards into my arms. I've noticed that the older they get, the less they trust that I will catch them. You would think the older they got, the more they would rely on past experience and know I would be there to catch them. Yet as Christians, we play the same trust/fall game with God day-in and day-out. Many of us spend our entire lives building man-made safety nets to catch us when we fall.

No doubt the Proverbs 31 woman planned ahead (Prov. 31:21). But one of her greatest attributes was her ability to look to the future with confidence. Proverbs 31:25 says, "she can laugh at the days to come." If only we could bottle her secret! Her contentment in life was not dependent on outside circumstances, but was a result of her trust in God. Can we really be content in life, regardless of the difficulties? We can't "laugh at the days to come" unless we can at least chuckle at today.

One ailment that prevents women from looking to the future with joy and confidence is the "if-only" syndrome. Here are some actual "if-onlys" I've heard through the years. My life would be abundant if only …

- ❑ my husband was a Christian.
- ☑ my husband was a spiritual leader.
- ❑ I had a job.
- ❑ I were in good health.
- ❑ I was married.
- ❑ I had not divorced.
- ☑ I could quit my job and stay home.
- ☑ my children were obedient.
- ❑ I had a better job.
- ☑ I made more money.
- ❑ I could meet the perfect guy.
- ❑ I had a good marriage.
- ❑ my kids walked with Christ.
- ❑ my prodigal would return.

If only, if only, if only … you get the picture. I have mumbled a couple of these "if-onlys." Check any that you may have voiced or with which you are currently struggling. The problem with "if-onlys" is that it makes the abundant life contingent on circumstances that are many times out of our control. There is certainly nothing wrong with having aspirations, but it becomes unhealthy when our happiness is tied to fulfilling them.

With what "if-onlys" do you currently struggle?

house, vocation

What is your prescription for the "if-onlys"? (check as many as you like)
- ❑ I call my best friend and recite them to her.
- ❑ I focus on the "if-only" *du jour* and try to make it a reality.
- ☑ I remind myself God is in control and happiness is a choice.
- ❑ I try to take the focus off myself and reach out to someone else in need.
- ❑ I get into God's Word to discover what He has to say about it.
- ☑ I charge up my credit card–a new pair of shoes cures everything.
- ☑ I hit the donut shop to binge away my worries.
- ❑ I hit the liquor store to escape from the uncertainties of life.
- ☑ I lift my "if-onlys" up to God and pour out my heart to Him.
- ☑ I pray about it.
- ❑ (List your own.) _____

Read Philippians 4:6-8. What is God's remedy for anxiety?

God's peace

How did this remedy compare with your choice?

right on track

What does thanksgiving have to do with laughing at the days to come?

take it easy, God's in control

What are some worthy things to dwell on, according to Philippians 4:8?

true, pure, just, lovely, good report

Read 1 Peter 5:7. Why should we trust God with our anxieties (worries)?

He truly cares

Do you really believe this? ☑ Yes ❑ No ❑ Can I get back to you on that?

The Proverbs 31 woman knew God loved her and had her best interests in mind. She never doubted He was in control of every detail of her life. When playing the trust/fall game with God, she didn't preoccupy herself with whether or not He would be there–she knew He would because He had always been there. With confidence, she never glanced back.

day 4
A Reflection of the Heart

After I spoke on the subject of "whining," a dear woman sent me a bumper sticker. It simply read, "Stop Global Whining"–a play on words, but I wonder if there's not a ring of truth to it! In Proverbs 31:26, we read, "She speaks with wisdom, and faithful instruction is on her tongue." Call it a hunch, but I doubt the Proverbs 31 woman was much of a whiner.

"She speaks with wisdom, and faithful instruction is on her tongue."

Proverbs 31:26

God's Word has plenty to say about the tongue, so it's no surprise that the Proverbs 31 woman had learned the art of "taming the tongue." In *The Message,* Eugene Peterson translates Proverbs 31:26 "When she speaks she has something worthwhile to say, and she always says it kindly." Ouch! Can we say that the majority of our conversations are "worthwhile" in nature and seasoned with godly wisdom? Just as important, are the majority of our words spoken in kindness?

Double ouch. In moments like this I wonder why God appointed me to write this book. Remember that catchy slogan, "Help! I've fallen and I can't get up"? I recently saw a T-shirt that read, "Help! I'm talking and I can't shut up!" Some of us just have the gift of gab—or is it? God keeps showing me that to speak with wisdom, I must first think before I speak.

When words are many, what is always around? (Prov. 10:19) ___Sin___

I can't help wondering, did the Proverbs 31 woman ever have a bad day? Did she speak with kindness 24 hours a day, 7 days a week? Was she ever overcharged on her phone bill and had to call and hold for 30 minutes just to straighten the mess out? Was it the classical music in the background that calmed her nerves?

Think of a recent frustrating experience. How did you respond? Was the "law of kindness" on your tongue? ❏ Yes ❏ No

Matthew Henry comments on Proverbs 31:26, "Her wisdom and kindness together put a commanding power into all she says; they command respect, they command compliance. She is full of pious religious discourse, and manages it prudently, which shows how full her heart is of another world even when her hands are most busy about this world."[1]

The virtuous woman commands respect, not as a result of an attitude, but as a result of her speech, reflecting the true nature of her heart. Her words "command compliance." If only we mothers could learn that! Wisdom is rarely present when we're screaming at our kids! Her knowledge of God and religion was abundant, yet she 'managed it prudently' and did not come across as a religious know-it-all to others."

What might Christians learn from this example when speaking to others about their faith?

think before speak

Can you think of three godly women who speak consistently with wisdom and kindness on their tongues? ☑ Yes ❑ No

As I think of godly women who are in the habit of consistently speaking with wisdom and kindness, they all have one thing in common: Each of these women exhibited a deep spirit of humility. Humility is an essential element in the pursuit to be a virtuous woman. The Hebrew word for *humility* is `anavah, which means "modesty, gentleness, and meekness." Displaying a spirit of humility comes naturally to someone who is in the habit of showing awe and reverence to God.

Someone who is humble understands that the only good in them comes from the grace of God. They are grateful for each day that God grants them and view it as a privilege that He placed them in the world for such a time as this. They realize that as long as they live, they have more to learn. They extend grace and mercy to others because they realize the value of God's grace and mercy in their own lives. They are deeply dependent on God's Word, and prayer is a part of their everyday lives.

Several of the godly women I know share testimonies to the fact that they used to be bitter in spirit until God's power and Truth transformed their lives. This should offer hope to each of us, that it's never too late for us. Luke 6:45b says, "For out of the overflow of his heart his mouth speaks."

Are the majority of your words spoken from an overflow of a grateful heart? ❑ Yes ❑ No *depends*

Close by writing a prayer expressing your gratefulness to God.

Lord, Thank you for listing to my hearts desires! Help me stay focused on You! not me

day 5
A Legacy Worth Leaving

Here we are on the final day! I so much hope God has used this study to show you that the qualities lending to the Proverbs 31 woman's virtuous standing are not out of reach for women today.

We began this study by discussing the legacy we might someday leave. How will we be remembered? Will we be remembered as women of worth, who recognized that true value only comes from God? as women of wisdom, who sought after "God sense," rather than the world's "good sense"? as women of purpose, who recognized their calling to fulfill the kingdom agenda as ambassadors of Christ? for our efficient, hardworking natures? for extending our hands to the needy? for our abilities to laugh at the days to come and to face the future with confident assurance? for speaking with wisdom and faithful instruction on our tongues? Most importantly, will we be remembered as women who feared the Lord by offering Him the awe and reverence He deserves?

How are you doing when it comes to the virtuous attributes we have covered? Mark an X on the line, with 10 being "Great!"

Worth:

0   5   10

Wisdom:

0   5   10

Purpose:

0   5   10

Efficiency/Hard worker

0   5   10

Gives to the needy

0   5   10

Laughs at the days to come

0	5	10

Speaks with wisdom and faithful instruction

0	5	10

What are your top three strengths and weaknesses?

_____

_____

_____

Write a prayer in the margin, asking God's direction as you seek to improve on your weaknesses.

Not by coincidence the Book of Proverbs begins and ends with "the fear of the Lord" (1:7; 31:30). We wrap up our study of Proverbs 31 with the final verses in the passage.

Her children arise and call her blessed; her husband also, and he praises her. "Many women do noble things, but you surpass them all. Charm is deceptive, and beauty is fleeting; but a woman who fears the Lord is to be praised. Give her the reward she has earned, and let her works bring her praise at the city gate" (Prov. 31:28-31).

As a review, describe what it means to fear the Lord:

_____

_____

Where do you rank yourself when it comes to "fear of the Lord"?

0	5	10

One can only imagine what awaits the woman who fears the Lord when she gets to heaven. Those who are Christians will stand before the

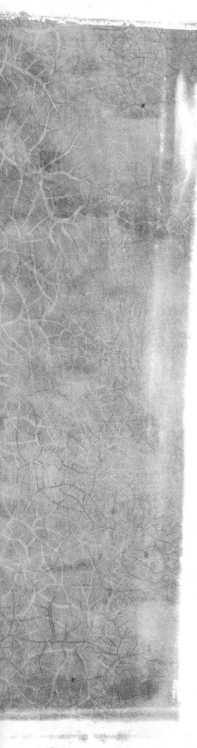

judgment seat of Christ (2 Cor. 5:10). Although their salvation is secure, their deeds on earth will be judged.

To understand this judgment, read 1 Corinthians 3:8-16.

In past years, I struggled to understand the purpose of believers going before the judgment seat of Christ. If our names are recorded in the Book of Life, why bother with judgment? What's all this about "suffering loss?" If heaven is a place where sadness is absent, how can one suffer loss?

What is the purpose of the rewards? (1 Cor. 3:13)

seprate our words, worthy, Not

I don't have all the answers, but God's Word speaks of the rewarding of crowns for certain accomplishments.

Read Revelation 4:9-11. What did the 24 elders do with their crowns?

Cast to the throne

The judgment will "bring to light" (1 Cor. 3:13) the quality of what we build for Christ and the crowns we receive will provide something to place at the feet of Jesus. With the elders we will cry out, "You are worthy, our Lord and God, to receive glory and honor and power, for you created all things, and by your will they were created and have their being" (v. 11).

Wow! If I don't have anything to lay at the feet of my Savior on that day, I will suffer loss. It won't be from envy, but from sheer regret that I failed to understand my purpose in life.

Recently my grandparents asked their four children to come for a discussion. Both grandparents are in their 80s and wanted to discuss their wills. They are both committed Christians and confident of their eternal home in heaven, so this was not an uncomfortable exercise. They discussed details such as who would get the land, their home, and many other belongings.

As I pondered the thought of leaving possessions behind to loved ones, I began to think of the many things people leave as an inheritance. I reflected on a day I had recently visited my grandparents home. My grand-mother had been diagnosed for a second time with cancer and wanted to share a timely verse with me. As she opened her worn Bible and turned the pages, I could see the margins filled with her notes. The pages were so worn from the turning that they were falling out. As she read the verse to me, I found myself thinking, "Dear God, may my Bible be as weathered and worn as my grandmother's." What a priceless possession. What a legacy to leave. Will my future grandchildren say the same of me?

A woman who fears the Lord will by her very nature, produce a legacy worth leaving. Gone are the days of SuperWoman–this woman is a super woman in the eyes of God. It's time for us to hang up our capes and rest in the assurance of God's unfailing love.

End the study by asking God to help you in the pursuit to become a virtu-ous woman. The study may be over, but the journey has just begun! This really is the great adventure.

[1] Bible Soft 22014 7th Ave. So.; Seattle, Wa 98198; 206/824-0547 *Matthew Henry's Commentary on the Whole Bible: New Modern Edition* electronic database; copyright © 1991 by Hendrickson Publisher, Inc. Used by permission. All rights reserved.

Virtuous Woman
Leader Guide

This leader guide will help you facilitate the six group sessions of the study. Sessions are planned to be one to one and one half hours in length. Feel free to adapt these suggestions to fit your group's needs and time constraints. I recommend an introductory session to start the study, but if you do not have time for an introductory meeting, distribute the books at least one week in advance and start with session 1.

Ask group members to consider inviting a neighbor, coworker, or friend who has not been in a Bible study. This study was written as a combination inreach/outreach tool for spiritual growth and is sensitive to varying levels of spiritual maturity. "SuperWoman" is a common struggle among women, and many would welcome the opportunity to be a part of a group that discusses the topic.

Introductory session (optional)
- Distribute the books and read aloud the Proverbs 31 passage (KJV) from page 5.
- Ask for volunteer comments and initial thoughts, after hearing the passage.
- Go over the passage again and have women in the group share different translations of some of the verses. (To have a *Living Bible* on hand for this exercise would be helpful.)
- If the group is large, break into smaller groups of

five to seven women and have one person read the Preface (the author's initial thoughts of the Proverbs 31 woman).
- Ask your group to share their impression of the Proverbs 31 woman (some women may be reading it for the first time!).
- Ask for volunteers to define the word *virtue* in their own words.
- Read the definition of *virtue* from the dictionary: "Conformity to a standard of right; morality; a particular moral excellence; a commendable quality or trait." (Webster's)
- Ask for volunteers to share a commendable quality present in the Proverbs 31 passage that they hope to cover during the study.

Closing exercise
Ask the group to share 'qualities' that might define the "world's ideal woman." Write the words on a marker board as they share them. Close by praying that God would assist each woman in the pursuit to become "the ideal woman" in His eyes.

Distribute a schedule with meeting times, what week will be covered, and the phone number and/or email address of the group leader. Consider assigning prayer partners to pray for each other and to call during the week to offer encouragement.

Session 1

The Ideal Woman

Introductory activity

- Divide up into groups of five to seven women and hand each group two or three magazines (fashion, decorating, fitness); give them five minutes to go through and tear out pages with pictures of women who define the world's definition of "the ideal woman." Have each group stand up and share five pictures, telling why they chose them.

Choose from any of the following questions for use in the group discussion. Note that I have furnished many more questions than you will have time to process in your group, so choose those you want to use. Don't worry if the group discussion only covers a small portion of the material.

For group discussion

Day 1 _____

- "You are who you've been becoming." Overall, is this thought comforting or (disturbing?) depends on day
- In regard to a legacy, what are some things you giving hope others will say about you? great friend
- In what ways do you hope your life will impact future generations?
- What were some qualities women were commended for in the obituaries you read?
- In your opinion, are most people more focused on the here and now, or molding a legacy for the future?

Day 2 _____

- What verses in Proverbs 31 do you find the most intimidating?
- In your opinion, what were the top five qualities that led to the Proverbs 31 woman's virtuous standing? Child call her blessed God fearing, wise + kind, faithful

Day 3 _____

- Including both positive and negative, what messages did you receive in your early years from family and friends in regard to becoming the "ideal woman"?
- What mediums does the world use to send messages in regard to the "ideal woman"?
- Read 1 Samuel 16:7. How do the messages you have received compare to God's standard?

Day 4 _____

- Look over the true/false chart on page 17. Ask for volunteers to share their responses.
- Can you look in a full-length mirror in your swimsuit and say, "I am fearfully and wonderfully made"? (Ps. 139:14).

Day 5 _____

- What are some things we can do to prepare our hearts to be fertile soil and receive the "scattered seed" in the weeks to come? prayer + Word
- What truth(s) did God sow in your heart during week 1? Constant pursue of Virtuous woman

97

Closing exercise

Ask volunteers to share a "fearful" moment in their lives–a heart-stopping type of situation. Ask them to describe what they were feeling at that moment (for example: breathless, speechless, shaking, screaming). If possible, write their words on a marker board as they express them. Explain that in week 2 they will discuss what it is to "fear the Lord." Ask them to pay close attention to the difference between the type of fear they described and the "fear of the Lord." Close in prayer.

Session 2
A Woman Who Fears the Lord

Introductory activity

(choose one)

- Ask members to share "miracles" they have witnessed or experienced. (Have them stick to first-hand experiences rather than hear-say.) Ask them what they felt toward God after the experience. Make the point that the new birth is a miracle to every believer. How do the feelings shared compare to what the Israelites may have felt toward God after witnessing many miracles?
- Ask group members to share life experiences in which they were in absolute awe of God (Example: childbirth, when they came to know Christ, and so forth.)

For group discussion

Day 1 _____

- Read over the definition of *fear of the Lord* on page 26. Have the women share an area they are strong in and an area they are weak in. Discuss practical ways to improve in the weak areas.

Day 2 _____

- Ask for two women to give a short (two minute) testimony of how they came to know Christ, the Author of Life.
- Ask for volunteers to share how they pictured themselves approaching the throne of grace (Hebrews 4:16) on page 27.
- Look back over your answers on page 28. What is your impression of the God of the Old Testament?

Day 3 _____

- Read Exodus 3:7-10. Does the passage portray a God of love and compassion or a God of judgment and wrath?
- Do you think that God is concerned with the suffering of His people today? Ask for volunteers to share a time in which God vividly showed Himself during a time of suffering.
- If you had been an Israelite during the time of the plagues, do you think you would have been supportive of Moses, or like many Israelites, angry with him?

Day 4 _____

- Read Exodus 4:10-12. Ask, "If you had been Moses, what do you think your response would have been?
- How are we as Christians similar to the Israelites when it comes to remembering our deliverance?

Day 5 _____

- Which of the verses on page 36 had the greatest impact on you and why?
- What truth(s) did God sow in your heart during week 2?

Closing exercise

Draw two columns on a marker board. Ask the women to share things that decrease their self-worth and list them in the first column. Have the women share some things that might boost their self-worth and list them in the second column. Tell them that week 3 will address the attribute of worth. Close in prayer.

Session 3
A Woman of Worth

Introductory activity (choose one)
- Show a clip from a movie such as "Forest Gump" or "Hope Floats" that depicts a modern-day "woman at the well." (Note: Movie clips can be a powerful medium to make a point. Please use discernment when choosing a clip and review it in advance to make sure that it would not offend anyone in your group. The clip should not run more than five minutes.
- Arrange for a willing volunteer from your group to share a testimony of a time when they felt like the Samaritan woman.
- Have everyone in the group list on slips of paper two accomplishments or achievements that have boosted their self-worth. Fold them up and turn them in to the leader. Read them one at a time and have the group try to guess who it is.

For group discussion

Day 1 _____

- Ask members to share examples of times when they have defined their worth by what they look like, what they do, or what others think of them.

Day 2 _____

- In what ways do people today hand down the false worth equations (worth = what you look like; worth = what you do; or worth = what others think) to their children or others? Are Christians also guilty of this?

Day 3 _____

- What truth(s) did God reveal to your heart in regard to the Samaritan woman?
- Ask the women whether they were able to list the things that have caused them guilt or shame (p. 45). Was there anything on their lists that still plagues them from time to time?

Day 4 _____

- Read John 4:39. What is "Living Water" a reference to?
- Is it possible for one to receive the Holy Spirit but fail to depend on His power? How does this hinder women from leaving the well?
- Discuss how Satan plays a part in women remaining at the well.
- Have you left the well? Can you honestly say, "it is finished"?

Day 5

- Re-read the opening paragraph on day 5. Discuss among your group possible reasons many Christian women will knowingly continue in sin.
- Have volunteers share some of their healthy forms of pleasure.
- Ask for volunteers to share a time when they chose "feeling good" over "doing good."
- Think back on the "lizard story" on page 46. Have you ever been an "almost dead" Christian? Was your life abundant?
- Ask for volunteers to share a time when they were able to choose God (doing good) over the world (feeling good) in a tempting situation.
- What truth(s) did God sow in your heart during week 3?

Closing exercise

Make two columns on the marker board. Ask the women to share examples of people who possess "godly wisdom." List the names in the first column. In the second column on the marker board, list examples of people who possess "worldly wisdom." Tell them that week 4 will discuss the attribute of "godly wisdom" and how it differs from "worldly wisdom." Close in prayer.

Session 4
A Woman of Wisdom

Introductory activity
(choose one)

- Ask for two women to come up and pose as a secular talk show host and the Proverbs 31 woman. Distribute three situations written on slips of paper to the remaining women and have them take turns asking the mock panel for advice. (Example: "I don't really love my husband anymore and I'm thinking about getting a divorce.") Tell the Proverbs 31 woman to offer godly wisdom and Oprah to offer worldly wisdom.
- Write two hot topics on the marker board (Example: homosexuality, sex before marriage) and make two columns. Ask the women to share godly wisdom and worldly wisdom in regard to each topic. List their responses in each column.

For group discussion

Day 1

- Have you ever had a mentor who models the Titus 2:3-5 passage?
- Have you ever mentored someone?
- How would having a mentor help women in the pursuit to gain wisdom?

Day 2

- Discuss the difference between worldly knowledge and godly wisdom. Which does the world esteem more?
- What must we do to obtain godly wisdom? (Jas. 1:5)

Day 3

- What precious jewels do you treasure?
- How might we go about handing down wisdom as a priceless commodity?

Day 4 _____

- Ask volunteers to share examples of a time when they prayed for wisdom but instead made a decision based on feelings.
- Which of the wisdom verses on page 61 impacted you most?
- Which of the folly verses on page 61 impacted you most?
- Have volunteers share examples of a situation in which they chose wisdom over folly.

Day 5 _____

- Put yourself in Abigail's place. How might you have responded to the situation at hand?
- What truth(s) did God sow in your heart during week 4?

Closing exercise

On a marker board write: "Our purpose in life is to _____." List group members' responses on the marker board, as they come up with them. Tell them that week 5 will examine the pursuit to become a woman of purpose. Close in prayer.

Session 5

A Woman of Purpose

Introductory activity

On the marker board or on a separate handout, have the women solve the following match-up from the Proverbs 31 passage:

merchant/businesswoman . . . . . .verse 10
wife . . . . .verse 13

manufacturer . . . . .verse 14
importer .verse 15
manager .verse 16
mother . . . . .verse 20
philanthropist/counselor . . . . . . .verse 24
realtor/farmer/gardener . . . . .verse 28

(Answers: wife-10; manufacturer-13; importer-14; manager-15; realtor/farmer/gardener-16; philanthropist/counselor-20; merchant/businesswoman-24; mother-28)

For group discussion

Day 1 _____

- What are some hats you currently wear? Which of your roles/hats bring you the greatest sense of purpose?
- Turn to page 69. Have your group read aloud Psalm 73:25-26 from the *New Living Translation*, substituting the words *they* and *were* with *I* and *was*. Share insights to this truth.
- Have the women share some things (if any) that keep God from being the number one desire of their hearts.

Day 2 _____

- What is the kingdom agenda? (To know Him and make Him known)
- Have the women brainstorm ways to fit the pursuit to "know God" into their Day-Timers (listen to worship music, have daily quiet times, read the Proverb that matches each day, have daily prayer time, attend church regularly, join a Bible study, attend a Christian conference or retreat, and so forth).

- Read Luke 10:38-42. Are you a Mary or a Martha? Are you more concerned with the work of the Lord or the Lord of the work?

Day 3 _____

- Have the women share ways to act as ambassadors (representatives) for Christ throughout their day.
- How does viewing those who do not know Christ as "sheep without a shepherd" fit into our job as ambassadors for Christ? What are some ways can we be sensitive to those who do not know the Good Shepherd?

Day 4 _____

- How can you bring your husband confidence and assure that he lacks nothing of value?
- How can you bring your husband "good and not harm"?
- Where you able to ask your husband the above questions?

Day 5 _____

- Have the mothers in your group share ways to speak to their children with "wisdom and faithful instruction" even when they (the moms) are angry or frustrated.
- How can we "watch over the affairs of our households"? (know child's peer group, monitor television time and content, rules when surfing the net, and so forth)
- Have mothers in the group share ways they are training their children to be ambassadors for

Christ and are teaching them the true purpose for their lives.
- What truth(s) did God sow in your heart during week 5?

Closing exercise

Ask volunteers to share about a time when they were chosen for something or awarded with an honor. Ask them how it felt to "surpass" others in their achievement. Tell them that week 6 will address four more attributes of the Proverbs 31 woman that, together with the rest, earned her recognition as a woman who "surpassed them all." Close in prayer.

Session 6
A Woman Who Surpasses Them All

Introductory activity

(choose one)
- Ask group members to share qualities for which they would want to be remembered. As they share them, list them on a marker board.
- Ask each group member to write a one- or two-paragraph memorial (how they want to be remembered), written from the perspective of someone close to them. Ask for volunteers to share what they wrote.

For group discussion

Day 1 _____

- Discuss the dangers of idle time. What can idle time lead to?
- How can idle time affect the virtuous attribute of efficiency?

- Ask volunteers to share practical ways to be more efficient.

Day 2 _____

- Read the Hebrew meaning of the words *needy* and *poor* on page 85. Do you know people who fit this category? Have you been needy or poor before?
- Share the differences between physically needy, emotionally needy, and spiritually needy.
- Share ways women today can extend their hand to the needy and poor.

Day 3 _____

- Look at the list of "if onlys" on page 88. Share "if onlys" to which you may have tied your happiness in the past.
- What are some remedies for the "if only" syndrome? How might these remedies help women to "laugh at the days to come"?

Day 4 _____

- How does humility affect our ability to speak with wisdom and kindness?
- Read Luke 6:45b. How do our words reflect the nature of our hearts? *garbage in, garbage out*

Day 5 _____

- Turn to page 93. Ask women to share their top three strengths in the pursuit to be virtuous.
- Ask volunteers to share one weakness and their plan to improve in that area.
- Discuss the concept of "suffering loss," as mentioned in 1 Corinthians 3:13-15.
- How might we make "fear of the Lord" an important part of the legacy we leave?
- What truth(s) did God sow in your heart during week 6?

Closing exercise

Encourage the women to schedule some time alone with God and review the truths He sowed in their hearts throughout the study. Just as the 24 elders laid their crowns at the feet of Jesus, might we all be willing to kneel at His feet and give ourselves over to Him in the pursuit to become virtuous women.

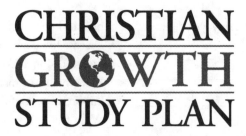

CHRISTIAN GROWTH STUDY PLAN

In the **Christian Growth Study Plan (formerly Church Study Course),** this book *The Virtuous Woman: Shattering the Superwoman Myth* is a resource for course credit in the subject area Personal Life of the Christian Growth category of plans. To receive credit, read the book, complete the learning activities, show your work to your pastor, a staff member or church leader, then complete the following information. This page may be duplicated. Send the completed page to:

Christian Growth Study Plan
• **One LifeWay Plaza** • **Nashville, TN 37234-0117**
• **FAX: (615)251-5067** • **Email: cgspnet@lifeway.com**
For information about the Christian Growth Study Plan, refer to the Christian Growth Study Plan Catalog. It is located online at www.lifeway.com/cgsp. If you do not have access to the Internet, contact the Christian Growth Study Plan office (1.800.968.5519) for the specific plan you need for your ministry.

The Virtuous Woman:
Shattering the Superwoman Myth
COURSE NUMBER: CG-0593

PARTICIPANT INFORMATION

Social Security Number (USA ONLY-optional)	Personal CGSP Number*		Date of Birth (MONTH, DAY, YEAR)
– –	–	–	– –

Name (First, Middle, Last)	Home Phone
	– –

Address (Street, Route, or P.O. Box)	City, State, or Province	Zip/Postal Code

Please check appropriate box: ❑ Resource purchased by self ❑ Resource purchased by church ❑ Other

CHURCH INFORMATION

Church Name

Address (Street, Route, or P.O. Box)	City, State, or Province	Zip/Postal Code

CHANGE REQUEST ONLY

☐ Former Name		
☐ Former Address	City, State, or Province	Zip/Postal Code
☐ Former Church	City, State, or Province	Zip/Postal Code

Signature of Pastor, Conference Leader, or Other Church Leader	Date

*New participants are requested but not required to give SS# and date of birth. Existing participants, please give CGSP# when using SS# for the first time. Thereafter, only one ID# is required. **Mail to:** Christian Growth Study Plan, One LifeWay Plaza, Nashville, TN 37234-0117. Fax: (615)251-5067.

Rev. 3-03